EMPTY WELL, THIRSTY HEART

Finding Wholeness in a Barren Land

MARK LEONARD

With Stephen W. Nance

Unless otherwise indicated, all Scripture quotations are from the Holy Bible, *New International Version*, © 1973, 1978, 1984 by International Bible Society.

Scripture quotations marked (NKJV) are from the *New King James Version*, © 1979, 1980, 1982 by Thomas Nelson, Inc.

EMPTY WELL, THIRSTY HEART: FINDING WHOLENESS IN A BARREN LAND

To contact the author, write to:
9445 E. Florida Ave.
Denver, CO 80247

ISBN 0-924748-33-8
Printed in the United States of America
© 2004 by Mark Leonard

Milestones International Publishers
4410 University Dr., Ste. 113
Huntsville, AL 35816
(256) 536-9402, ext. 234   Fax: (256) 536-4530
www.milestonesinternationalpublishers.com

Cover design by: Kirk Douponce/UDG DesignWorks
www.udgdesignworks.com

1 2 3 4 5 6 7 8 9 10 11 / 09 08 07 06 05 04

DEDICATION

I would like to dedicate this book to my daughter Sophia and my wife Helena, for whom I hope to always be a living well full of love and encouragement. It is my prayer that they grow in love, fulfillment, and happiness, and in turn become wells of life to others.

TABLE OF CONTENTS

Part One:
Into the Desert—The Nurturing Years

Part Two:
Turning Point—Self-Discovery

Part Three:
Out of the Desert—The Journey to Healing and Freedom

FOREWORD

Having just read this book, I can honestly say that it goes beyond Promise Keepers. This is a message for women; it is a message to mothers. This is a message for men; it is a message to fathers. Understand the power of your words. Understand the power of affirmation. Understand the power of making yourself available and forever ending the effects of the tragedy of what Mark calls the "empty well syndrome."

I believe this book has the power to transform generations. It is awesome—creative and original and desperately needed. I am truly proud, humbled, and honored to be a part of this project. I wholeheartedly endorse this book because I know that if you are man or woman enough to grasp the truth within these pages, you will literally break the generational curses of the empty well syndrome in your family line. This is part of what Promise Keepers has played a small role in: teaching men, teaching fathers, the power of making themselves available to their children, to their wives, to their churches, and to their communities, and understanding the detriment of being invisible to the needs around us.

This book touches the very heart of the American family. Have you ever wondered why Almighty God spoke audibly, stating, "This is my beloved Son, in whom I am well pleased" (Matthew 3:17 KJV)? Jesus needed affirmation. This Father and Son modeled it for all of us. If we could offer affirmation and support and love, we would create a foundation or a pathway to tremendous healing in the family today. Our actions have the power to literally change negative reactions into positive results. The power of believing in and building up future generations in the family unit is an untapped power today.

I encourage you to prayerfully read this book, take its message to heart, and share it with others. Expect to be challenged, expect to be humbled, expect to be healed. This book will force you to look at your life and then compel you to live free. You may cry, but in the end you will conquer what has conquered you for so long. Perhaps your well has been empty for years, and you have been searching for a fill. Get ready, for the water is here!

Coach Bill McCartney

Part One:

INTO THE DESERT—
THE NURTURING YEARS

Chapter One

ALL YOU NEED IS LOVE

One of the saddest tragedies in life is a heart left barren, the child in us, whatever our age, ignored, punished, and tormented, even as we search continually, desperately, and unsuccessfully for fulfillment. Hopes crushed, dreams shattered, and spirit broken by repeated rejection, we stumble aimlessly through an emotional desert, a loveless, barren wasteland of parched earth, dry streambeds, and empty wells, scrambling frantically for an oasis, a spring, or a pool—any source of water where we can drink our fill, slake our thirst, and be satisfied.

Nothing hurts like rejection. No pain equals the gut-wrenching agony of discovering that the person who cannot or will not give you the love and affirmation you seek is the very person you need and want it from the most. All your life you have been searching for love, craving it, doing everything you know to do trying to win the attention, the approval, the love you so desperately need. You have tried again and again. And you have failed—again and again.

Love defines who we are as human beings.

Nothing drives human activity and endeavor more than the thirst for love. Because of love, empires have risen and fallen and wars have been fought. Love has inspired some of mankind's greatest art, literature, and music. I believe that it is reasonable to say that virtually everything we do in life is motivated in one way or another by our need to love or be loved. In a very real sense, love defines who we are as human beings. To paraphrase the apostle Paul, without love we have nothing and are nothing.

So how much is love worth, anyway?

What would you give up for love?

Would you give up your career?

Edward VIII, king of England, gave up his throne in 1936 to marry Wallis Simpson, an American and a commoner.

Would you give up your possessions?

Saint Francis of Assisi, born to an affluent Italian family, sold all his possessions in 1204 and devoted himself to repairing churches. This decision cost him his friends and his inheritance, for his father disowned him. Four years later he answered a call from God to leave everything and follow Him. Taking the call literally, Francis discarded his shoes, donned a simple gray garment with a rope belt, and established the

Franciscan Order, a monastic order committed to a complete vow of poverty. Throughout the remainder of his short life, Francis was known for his humility, his evangelistic preaching, and his loving devotion to God.

Would you give up your life?

In 1956, Jim Elliott and four fellow missionaries landed their pontoon plane on the Cururay River deep in eastern Ecuador. Their plan was to carry the Gospel of Christ to the Auca Indians, a previously unreached people group. Days later their spear-riddled bodies were found near their landing site. They had been killed by the very people they had come to reach. For love of the Gospel and the Auca Indians of Ecuador, Jim Elliott and his colleagues were willing to give their lives.

How far would you go to demonstrate your love?

Would you build a monument?

India's Taj Mahal, the most well-preserved and architecturally beautiful tomb in the world, was built in the seventeenth century by a Muslim emperor as a tribute and memorial to his beloved second wife, who died in childbirth.

Would you always be there, no matter what?

Fred Smith, an author and business leader, relates this story:

> One of my treasured memories comes from a doughnut shop in Grand Saline, Texas. A young farm couple was sitting at the table next to mine. He was wearing overalls and she a gingham dress. After finishing their doughnuts, he got up to pay the bill, and I noticed she did not get up to follow him.

But then he came back and stood in front of her. She put her arms around his neck, and he lifted her up, revealing that she was wearing a full body brace. He lifted her out of her chair and backed out the front door to the pickup truck, with her hanging from his neck. As he gently put her into the truck, everyone in the shop watched. No one said anything until a waitress remarked, almost reverently, "He took his vows seriously."[i]

Until we know we are loved, we cannot truly love someone else.

Would you do something recklessly extravagant?

Mark 14:3-9 (NKJV) tells of a woman who broke open a jar of perfume worth more than 300 denarii and poured all its contents on Jesus' head. Three hundred denarii—equivalent to a year's wages for a common laborer—gone in a moment. Pretty extravagant love!

What would you give to know that you are loved?

Everybody Needs Love

Our need to be loved is perhaps the single greatest need in our lives. It is universal. Regardless of our culture or ethnicity, every one of us needs to know that we are loved. This need outweighs our need to give love because until we know we are loved, we cannot truly, fully love someone else.

Love fulfills one of our most basic needs, and that need is inborn. Babies deprived of love, physical affection, and human contact such as holding, cuddling, and being talked to become withdrawn emotionally and even become lethargic. Deprived of these things long enough, they will even die.

In the 1940s, psychologist Abraham Maslow developed a theory that all human behavior is an effort to satisfy unfulfilled needs, and that lower needs take priority over higher needs. In this "hierarchy of needs," the lower or most basic needs must be satisfied before the higher ones can be addressed. Most basic of all are *physiological needs*: food, water, breathable air, sleep—those things that are necessary for physical survival. At the next level are *safety needs* such as shelter, security, stability, freedom from fear, anxiety, and chaos, and the need for structure, law, and order. Just above safety needs are *belongingness and love needs*: friendship, belonging to a group, giving and receiving love. One level higher are the *esteem needs*: self-respect, self-esteem, achievement, recognition. Finally, at the top is the level of *self-actualization needs*: the need to reach for one's full potential as a person. This level takes in such things as truth, justice, wisdom, and meaning. People at this level are free to express who they really are: musicians must make music, artists must paint, writers must write.

Needs at any level that remain unmet hinder a person's progress to the next level. A starving man has one thing on his mind: finding food. Someone dying of thirst will forego every other need until that basic physiological need for water is satisfied. In the same way, people who lack love or a sense of being loved will have difficulty finding fulfillment at the esteem and self-actualization levels. They may even try extra hard in those areas in an effort to compensate for the love deficiency in their lives. Frequently, such people become overachievers or workaholics, driven to succeed and excel in hopes of filling the love-shaped hole in their hearts. Others adopt annoying, obnoxious, or even self-destructive behavior patterns—anything to get attention and, hopefully, the love they crave. Some people starved of love simply give up trying to fill that void and settle into unfulfilled lives of disappointment, disillusionment, loneliness, and, often, bitterness.

No matter who we are or where we come from, we all need love. Male or female, rich or poor, young or old, ignorant or educated, it makes no difference; the need for love is the common bond we all share. We need the love of family, we need the love of friends, and we need the love of God. When we don't have it, or feel that we don't, our lives are empty and unfulfilling. Like a V8 engine that is only firing on five cylinders, a life without love somehow doesn't "work" right. Without love, our lives are missing a critical design component.

We Are Designed for Love

From the very beginning God, our Master Designer, built into us the capacity—and the need—for love. The Bible says that God *is* love and that He created man in His own image. He who *is* love created us to be like Him. God, the Great Lover, designed us to love and to be loved. In this, we are unique among all of God's creations.

Because God is love, everything He does is an expression of His love nature. When God created the angels and all the heavenly host, He was expressing His love. When He created the Earth and all the abundance of life that inhabits it, He was expressing His love. Finally, when God created mankind, the crowning glory of His creativity, He was expressing His love. But something was different this time. When it came to man,

God added something extra. He poured His image, His like-ness—His *love*—into us, giving us the ability, alone of all His creatures, to love Him in return.

God is complete and sufficient within Himself, lacking nothing, needing nothing, and deficient in nothing. Why then did He create us in the first place? Let's look at it this way. God is love, and it is the nature of love to express itself. God expressed His love in acts of creation. It is also the nature of love to desire to be loved in return. Where in all His creation could God find that love? He couldn't get it from the sun, moon, stars, and planets because they are nothing more than balls of noble gases or lifeless rock and metal ore. He couldn't get it from the animals because they live

> *We are designed for love and are incomplete without it.*

and survive on instinct but have no capacity for genuine love. He couldn't get it from the angels because, even though they praise Him and serve Him and honor Him and glorify Him, they are simply doing what He created them to do. Nowhere does the Bible say either that the angels were created in God's image or that they have the capacity to love Him as we under-stand the word. Something inside God wanted someone who not only *could* love Him but could also freely *choose* to do so.

When God created us in His image, He imparted to us the capacity to receive, understand, and appreciate His love, as well as the ability to love Him in return. He also fashioned in us the hunger—the drive—to love and to be loved on the human level. As the Scriptures make clear, we are designed for love and are incomplete without it:

The LORD God said, "It is not good for the man to be alone. I will make a helper suitable for him."…So the LORD God caused the man to fall into a deep sleep; and while he was sleeping, he took one of the man's ribs and closed up the place with flesh. Then the LORD God made a woman from the rib he had taken out of the man, and he brought her to the man. The man said, "This is now bone of my bones and flesh of my flesh; she shall be called 'woman,' for she was taken out of man." For this reason a man will leave his father and mother and be united to his wife, and they will become one flesh (Genesis 2:18, 21-24).

I am not suggesting that unmarried people are in any way "incomplete" if they do not have a spouse to love and who will love them in return. My point is that human love—between husband and wife, between parents and children, between siblings, between friends—is part of God's design for us. Without love a vital part of our "machinery" is missing and we cannot function properly. Love reassures us that our life has meaning.

From the very beginning, God put inside each of us a yearning to know that we are important to someone else, a "need to be needed," if you will. Men, for example, have an innate need to be needed and loved as the "conqueror," the "protector," the strong one. They need their loved ones to love them and to look at them that way. Women need to be needed and loved not just for their capacity to bear children, but also for their minds and their intellects, their talents, gifts, and abilities. They need to know that they are important for more than just their physical attributes.

How would you feel if your spouse or your children conveyed the attitude that they did not need you? If your parents acted as though they could get along fine without you? If your boss came to you and said, "I'm sorry, but we won't be needing your services anymore"? If you worked tirelessly and selflessly day in and day out for the sake of someone you love only to discover that he or she has never noticed it? How would you feel?

Love is to our human spirit what water is to our physical body.

Maybe something like this *has* happened to you. Maybe you are sitting there nodding your head, thinking, *Yep, I know just what that's like.* Who of us at one time or another has never experienced rejection or a feeling of being unloved? It's like getting kicked in the gut, isn't it?

We all have a need to be needed, an insatiable craving to know that someone loves us, cares about us,

and appreciates us. Love is to our human spirit what water is to our physical body. Most of us cannot survive more than two or three days without water. Without water, our body starts to shut down. We start to feel weak and dizzy. We get a headache and cramps in our arms and legs. Our lips and tongue dry out We become restless or irritable. In advanced dehydration, our blood pressure drops and we experience fainting spells. We get a bloated stomach. We suffer severe muscle contractions in our arms, legs, stomach, and back, and eventually go into convulsions. Finally, we suffer heart failure.

In a similar manner, without love our spirit becomes parched and brittle. Prolonged deprivation leads to a pronounced state of spiritual and emotional dehydration. We withdraw into ourselves and gradually lose the ability and the will to respond to others' attempts to draw us out or relate to us.

God created us with the need for love and affirmation. While that need is lifelong, it is especially critical when we are growing up. The more loved and affirmed we are as children and youth, the more loving and affirming we will be as adults. How successful and well-adjusted we are as adults depend in no small measure on the love and affirmation we receive as children. If we are deprived of these things, we will grow up to be emotionally dysfunctional.

Whenever any of our basic love needs go unmet, we devote all our time, energy, and effort to fill those needs any way we can. Consciously or subconsciously, everything we do is geared to that end. We are like people dying of thirst in a barren land. Without love and affirmation, our life during these nurturing years becomes like a journey through the desert in a desperate search for water.

Finding Water

Water is essential for human survival. It is no coincidence that all major civilizations have grown up around rivers or other abundant sources of water. Think about Egypt's Nile River, Mesopotamia's Tigris and Euphrates rivers, Europe's Danube River, Italy's Tiber River, England's River Thames, the Ganges River of India, the Yangtze River of China, and South America's Amazon River.

People who inhabit barren, arid parts of the world have become experts in finding water in unexpected places. Their survival depends on it. Australia's indigenous people, the Aborigines, know how to take a hollow reed, insert it into the dry ground of the outback, and extract water by mouth as through a straw. Nomadic peoples of the African and Arabian deserts have known for millennia how to navigate the trackless sands and barren rock to locate every oasis that will provide life-sustaining water for themselves, their families, and their flocks and herds.

The northern part of Mexico's Yucatan Peninsula is low and relatively flat, with no surface rivers or streams. Yet, the first Western explorers to arrive there encountered a long-established indigenous culture centered around water. In the Yucatan, abundant fresh water lies below ground because of subterranean rivers that flow beneath the peninsula. In many places, water has over the millennia filtered through the limestone to form an intricate network of caves and *cenotes*, or underground chambers that contain permanent water. Some cenotes are vertical, water-filled shafts, usually of fairly small diameter, while others are caves that contain pools or underwater passages.

Currently, around 1,000 of these cenotes have been located, but they represent only about 25 percent of the estimated total number. Fresh water from these cenotes has sustained human life on the Yucatan for centuries, beginning with the Mayans as early as 3,000 years ago. Except for a few places in Florida and the island of Cuba, the Yucatan is the only place in the world where such a subterranean water system is found.

Because water is so central to life, it is often used as a symbol for life. The Bible frequently refers to water in this way. From the Pishon, Gihon, Tigris, and Euphrates rivers that watered the Garden of Eden in Genesis, to the Gospel of John's reference to Jesus as the *"living water,"* to the *"river of the water of life"* in the book of Revelation, the Scriptures are full of passages where water symbolizes life.

The cenotes of Yucatan are a kind of natural well that serve as access points to the fresh water below the surface. In other places where surface water is scarce and no river is nearby, people drill wells to tap into the water in the aquifer many feet underground. Sometimes they build or carve out cisterns to catch rainwater. Entire communities have sprung up around artesian springs, where immense underground pressures have forced water to the surface spontaneously. One thing all these have in common is that they provide access points for the water needed to nourish and sustain life.

Where Are *Your* Wells?

Most Americans today live in cities and have access to city water systems. All you have to do to get water is turn on the tap. Many people in smaller communities and in rural areas rely on wells for their water supply. I am sure we all remember the classic image of a well: a round wall of wood or stone surrounding the well itself, with a wooden framework and a rope and bucket for drawing up water by hand. Modern wells are somewhat different. First, a hole is drilled into the ground to whatever depth is necessary to reach water, and then a pump is installed to pump the water out of the well and into the house. The entire system is then capped and sealed for protection.

Like any other water system, a well is not itself the source of the water; it simply gives us access to the source. Want a drink of water? Go to the well. Need water for a shower? Go to the well. Need water for cooking or for washing clothes? Go to the well and draw whatever you need, whenever you need it.

All You Need Is Love

Just as water is central to our physical life, love is central to our spiritual and emotional lives. Without water we will die in less than a week. Without love our spirits will dry up and we will die emotionally. Water refreshes and rejuvenates our body, helps wash out toxins, and promotes general physical health. In the same way, love energizes and replenishes us emotionally and nourishes our spirits. It washes away the toxins of negativity, defeat, and discouragement that we pick up in the world and gives us the courage and confidence to keep going. Love lifts us up. I have always liked the Joe Cocker song, "Up Where We Belong," that says:

> Love lift us up where we belong
>
> Where the eagles fly on a mountain high
>
> Love lift us up where we belong
>
> Far from the world below
>
> Where the clear winds blow.[2]

If you did a self-examination of your life, could you honestly say that you know what it means to love and to be loved? When you need water you go to the well and draw from the source. Where do you go when you need love? Where do you turn to quench your emotional thirst? Who are the emotional "wells" in your life? Who do you go to when you need to draw from the waters of love, comfort, acceptance, approval, or healing? Your parents? Your grandparents? Your spouse? Your children? An aunt or an uncle? Your boss? Your pastor? A close friend? What is your source for satisfying your love and belongingness needs?

All of us have emotional "wells" in our lives, people we turn to and depend on to supply the emotional underpinnings of love and affirmation we need. For most of us, our main well is our parents. As children, we naturally looked to Mom and Dad for expressions of love and approval, longing to hear them say in word and action, "I love you! I'm proud of you! You are very special to me!" If you grew up in such a home, where your parents' well was always full and you could draw refreshing draughts of love and affirmation whenever you needed them, you are truly blessed.

For many of us, however, our experience was different. Maybe you grew up in a blended family with a stepparent who abused you, or a single-parent home broken by divorce. Maybe you never knew your father and your mother was always too drunk or too strung out on crack to notice you were there. Maybe your strongest childhood memory is of living in fear every day, never knowing when your dad was going to explode and start punching you or your brother or your sister or your mom. How well you remember crying yourself to sleep night after night amidst the pain of your blackened eye and split lip and the sound of your mother getting slammed around in the next room. Even worse was having to go to school the next day and tell all your friends that you "fell down."

Just as painful are the wounds that cannot be seen from the outside, the wounds inflicted on your spirit by harsh or thoughtless words, denial of love or affirmation, or constant criticism. Emotional starvation is just as much a form of abuse as is a physical beating, but the damage inflicted may be much worse. Physical bruises heal in a matter of days, but emotional bruises may last a lifetime.

Maybe your mother or father was fundamentally incapable of relating to your emotional needs or recognizing your achievements. Nothing you did was ever good enough. You worked your tail off to get a "B" in math and the only comment you heard was, "Why didn't you get an 'A'?" No matter how hard you tried, you could never please them. Regardless of your efforts, you never felt loved or appreciated or approved of. If you ever tried to talk to them openly about your feelings and how they were hurting you, all you accomplished was to make them angry. Then they gave you the big lecture about how ungrateful you were for all the sacrifices they had made for you.

Our parents represent the first stage of love training in our lives.

That child inside each of us—the child who needs love and approval and affirmation—never grows up and never goes away. You may be grown, married, and with children of your own and still be trying desperately to please your parents, to elicit from them even just one gesture or one word that shows they love you and care about you.

We all have emotional wells we draw from, but the problem is that as children we usually have no control over who our wells are. The quality of our wells as children directly affects the kind of adults we become. Our natural tendency is to treat others the way we were treated, to teach them the things we were taught, and to give them what was given to us. If your parents gave love freely and expressed it openly, chances are you do too. On the other hand, if your parents did not know how to love you as a child, you are probably still thirsty for that love today and may have trouble understanding how to love your own children. Our parents represent the first stage of love training in our lives. Failure to get it there can establish a pattern that may leave us emotionally thirsty and malnourished for the rest of our lives.

Looking for Love

If we cannot get the love we need from the traditional "wells" in our lives, we will start looking elsewhere. Sometimes we don't even know what we are looking for. All we know is that we have an emptiness inside that must be filled, a pain that must be soothed. What causes a young child to act out for attention? What causes a teenager or young adult to become sexually promiscuous or turn to drugs or alcohol? It is the need to fill their lives with something that makes them feel good.

No matter who we are or how old we are, we all have the need to feel good. Just as lack of water will eventually cause severe physical pain, absence of love causes emotional pain just as acute. That pain drives us to seek relief any way we can. Once we find someone or something that makes us feel good—even for a little while—we grab hold and hang on for dear life, whether it's healthy for us or not. All we want is for the pain to go away. There is a love-shaped hole in our hearts, and we will try to fill it with booze, drugs, sex, thrill-seeking, risk-taking, and generally dangerous living—anything we think will ease our pain.

Our quest to feel good is really nothing other than the search for love. As long as we feel unloved, we cannot truly love or feel good about ourselves. Lack of self-love often leads to self-destructive behavior. It also makes it impossible for us to love anyone else the way we should. If we cannot love someone else, we cannot love God, from whom love comes in the first place.

All You Need Is Love

Can you see how important love is? Can you understand why it is so important to draw from full, healthy wells? Love is central to our lives and to all our relationships with both God and man. Someone once asked Jesus to name the greatest commandment. In answering, Jesus went one better:

Jesus replied: "'Love the Lord your God with all your heart and with all your soul and with all your mind.' This is the first and greatest commandment. And the second is like it: 'Love your neighbor as yourself.' All the Law and the Prophets hang on these two commandments" (Matthew 22:37-40).

It all boils down to love God and love your neighbor as yourself.

Love God and love your neighbor as yourself; that's what it all boils down to. Jesus said that all the Law and the Prophets hang on those two commandments. What He meant is that everything in God's Word centers on love: love for God and love for others as for ourselves. In other words, everything we find in the Bible is a fleshing out, a living out, of these two commandments.

Love is eternal because it comes from God who is eternal. Our capacity to love and be loved originates with Him. John, one of Jesus' apostles, stated it this way:

Dear friends, let us love one another, for love comes from God. Everyone who loves has been born of God and knows God. Whoever does not love does not know God, because God is love. This is how God showed his love among us: He sent his one and only Son into the world that we might live through him. This is love: not that we loved God, but that he loved us and sent his Son as an atoning sacrifice for our sins. Dear friends, since God so loved us, we also ought to love one another. No one has ever seen God; but if we love one another, God lives in us and his love is made complete in us (1 John 4:7-12).

If you are in the middle of a love drought and your well does not seem to satisfy, go straight to the source. God is love, and He can supply the love you lack in your life. His love can bring healing to your spirit, fill that love-shaped hole in your heart (which is really a God-shaped hole anyway), and enable you to love yourself, thus making it possible to love Him in return and to love others as well.

When you go to your well you expect to be able to draw good water from it. What if that doesn't happen? What if your well is empty? One of the reasons many people have trouble loving God or feeling loved by God is because they have never felt loved by their parents and consequently are unable to love themselves. The well they go to for love is empty, and they go away empty-handed again and again and again.

We who are parents have a responsibility to be living examples to our children because the way they view us is the way they view authority. The same is true for us in our relationship with our parents. Our attitude toward God, whom the Bible calls our "Father," will likely reflect the model of parenthood we saw in our own parents. Were your parents loving and affirming, accepting you as you were but always challenging you to be your best? Were you comfortable and confident in their love and approval? If so, you will probably look at God the same way. Were your parents harsh and demanding, impossible to please and never satisfied with you? Were they violent and abusive? Were they cold, distant, and indifferent, always too caught up in their own affairs to notice you? Then you will probably see God that way too.

It doesn't stop there. If our attitude reflects what we saw in our parents, then our children's attitude will reflect what they see in us. When your children look at you, what do they see? What kind of a well are you to your children? This question is appropriate for parents of any age. Your children may be grown, but they will never outgrow the need for your love, affirmation, acceptance, and approval. Do they have it, and do they know they have it? When they come to draw water from your well, will they be satisfied or will they go away thirsty still?

A child's nurturing years should be a green, fertile valley filled with love, joy, laughter, affirmation, growth, fulfillment, and a growing sense of self-worth, confident in the love of family and of God. Far too many children, however, deprived of love, wander instead through a dry, bleak, and barren land-scape, parched and thirsty, searching endlessly for something they can never find.

Which of these pictures describes you? Which one describes your children? No matter who you are, the presence or absence of love in your life will make the difference between whether you are sitting comfortably, content, filled, and satisfied, or standing in the middle of the desert screaming for attention.

Endnotes

1. Quoted in Rodney L. Cooper, *Holman New Testament Commentary: Mark.* (Nashville: Holman Reference, Broadman and Holman Publishers, 2000) p. 233.

2. Joe Cocker and Jennifer Warnes, "Up Where We Belong" (Nitzche/ Jennings/Sainte-Marie). Album: *An Officer and a Gentleman* soundtrack. 1982.

Chapter Two

DADDY, I'M BEGGING FOR YOUR ATTENTION!

Imagine for a moment that your children are at your funeral sharing their memories of you. What would you want them to say? How would you like to be remembered?

"I wish Dad had spent less time at the office and more time at home."

"Dad was always more interested in golf than he was in me."

"No matter how hard I tried, nothing I did was ever good enough for Mom."

"I can't remember the last time Dad told me he loved me."

"I wish that Mom would have told me just once that she was proud of me."

"Mom never had time for me. She was always too busy with church stuff."

"I lived in fear whenever Dad was around because I never knew when he would blow up."

"The only time Mom ever paid attention to me was when she was yelling at me or criticizing me."

"Would it have been so hard for Dad to let me know every now and then that I had done something right?"

"Nothing that was important to me ever mattered to him."

"Mom never approved of me or anything I did."

"I don't think Mom ever really understood me—or cared."

"Dad never knew who I was."

"I always knew Mom loved me. She told me every day and showed it in her actions."

"Dad was always there for me when I needed him."

"No matter what else she was doing, if I needed something, Mom always made me feel like I was the most important person in the world."

"The times I remember most are the times when Dad took me fishing—just the two of us."

"I remember how Mom never got impatient with me when she was teaching me something new."

"I will never forget graduation day, when Dad put his arm around me and said, 'I am so proud of you.'"

"Mom was always quick to praise and slow to criticize. That's one of the things I loved about her."

Daddy, I'm Begging for Your Attention!

"If I have one wish, it is to be as good a father to my children as my father was to me."

As parents, our every word, gesture, facial expression, and action sends a message to our children. Everything we do communicates to them how we feel about them. Actions do speak louder than words. Our children will draw conclusions based more on what we do than on what we say. What kind of parenting legacy are we leaving behind? What seeds, for good or ill, are we sowing for the next generation to reap?

Actions do speak louder than words.

"Look at Me, Daddy, Look at Me!"

Children crave attention; it is part of their nature. It is also critical for their survival, particularly at young ages. Newborn infants cannot do anything for themselves. Without someone to feed them, change them, and care for them, they will die. A two-year-old does not understand how dangerous it is to walk into the street. Left outside unattended, he or she is headed for serious injury or worse.

We all have an inborn need for attention, and that need never goes away. It may change and mature through the years, but we never outgrow our need to be noticed, our need to be needed, our need to know that we are important to somebody else. Inside each of us is a yearning to know that we have a place in someone else's life, that we *belong*. As long as that need is unmet, we will do everything we can to fill it. People who are deprived of attention as children will still seek it as adults, and they may often do so in childish ways.

The first and most natural place that we look for the attention we need is from our parents. Normally, they are the first humans we have contact with after we are born, and the first that we form any bonds with. It is perfectly normal that we would look to mom and dad for love, approval, comfort, instruction, and encouragement. Our parents are the first "wells" that we dip into for the emotional waters that we need to survive and thrive. What we find there will in large part determine how we experience the world around us. If the well is full, we too will be full and satisfied, secure in the knowledge that we can draw from that well whenever we need. Life for us will be like a fertile, well-watered garden of joy and delight. A dry well, on the other hand, will turn our life into a parched, arid desert with barren ground all around.

A parent's response can make all the difference in the life of a child. What is the first thing a child says who has just learned to ride his bicycle without training wheels? "Look at me, Daddy, look at me! I'm riding all by myself!" Or, "Mommy, look at me! Look what I can do!" The child has just dipped into the well. What kind of water will come out? This is where the parent can make or break the child's spirit. Suppose the father or mother says, "That's wonderful! Great job! I knew you could do it! I'm proud of you." Refreshing waters of affirmation and approval send the child away satisfied and happy. On the other hand, suppose the parent says, without even looking up, "That's nice," and continues with what he or she is doing. What message does that send the child? Bitter water (or no water) from the well leaves the child feeling, *Nothing that I do matters. Mom (or Dad) doesn't care anyway.*

Daddy, I'm Begging for Your Attention!

A child's desire for attention is an insatiable craving that must be satisfied one way or another. If positive steps don't work, negative steps will do. All that matters is getting attention—any kind of attention—from the adults who are most important in a child's life. A young child's reasoning operates on a very basic and often subconscious level: *If Mommy won't notice me when I'm good, maybe she'll notice me when I'm bad. I may get in trouble, but at least she'll notice me.*

This is one reason so many children act out in public places. They are crying out to be noticed. By their behavior they are screaming desperately, "Pay attention to me!" Our need for attention is so vital to our overall well-being that not having it is a form of emotional starvation. Deliberately depriving someone of it constitutes emotional abuse.

Attention Deprivation Disorder

More and more children in our country today are being diagnosed with Attention Deficit Disorder (ADD), also known as Attention Deficit/Hyperactivity Disorder (ADHD). Children with this condition have abnormally short attention spans, experience learning problems, and have difficulty both concentrating and completing projects. They are also hyperactive and engage in impulsive, often disruptive behavior.

There is another kind of "ADD" that I believe has reached epidemic proportions. We could call it "Attention *Deprivation* Disorder." Our country is full of attention-deprived, emotionally starved kids, and their numbers are growing. They come from every social and economic class. Many have affluent parents who try to substitute money and "things" for genuine love and affection. Others have parents who are too career-focused to have time for them. Lots of middle- and lower-class kids, especially those in single-parent families, have too much unsupervised time on their hands because their parents have to work long hours or even two or three jobs just to make ends meet. Then there are the kids whose parents are wasted on crack or heroin or alcohol, so lost in a drug-induced haze that they are hardly aware that their children are even there.

Our country is full of attention-deprived, emotionally starved kids.

One of the largest groups of "ADD" kids is those whose parents, one or the other or both, were "ADD" themselves. Attention-deprived children usually grow into attention-deprived adults and pass their "ADD" to their children, not because they want to, but because they don't know how not to. Often, "ADD" parents have learned so well how to put up guards and defenses against future hurts that they shut themselves off emotionally from everybody, including their own children. Because as children they never received or saw modeled the love and attention they craved, they do not know how to give it as adults.

What are the symptoms of "Attention Deprivation Disorder"? They are many, and they vary from person to person and situation to situation. I've already mentioned one of the most common: acting out in public, making a scene in order to get attention. More drastic measures might include joining a gang or taking on potentially life-threatening activities such as extreme sports or reckless risk-taking. Many desperate kids are so starved for attention that they even attempt suicide in an effort to get it.

Daddy, I'm Begging for Your Attention!

In addition to acting out, risk-taking, and self-destructive behavior, attention deprivation can cause deep hurt, sorrow, anger, bitterness, desperation, and despair, giving rise to an overall sense of futility and worthlessness. All this can lead to rebellion, where children reject the beliefs and values of their parents, become resentful of authority, and get in trouble with the law.

There is another side to the coin, however. Many children, rather than rebelling against their parents, try to become just like them. In their craving for love and attention, they will do anything they can in an effort to please their parents and win their approval. They may work hard to excel academically because they think it will please their parents. They may strive to excel in sports for the same reason. They may become apple-polishers, sucking up to their parents at every opportunity. They may become perfectionists or even workaholics, always pushing, always striving, always intensely self-critical because they want so much to please mom or dad and win even one word of praise, one iota of attention, a single crumb of affection. They may take a particular job, choose a particular career, attend a particular college, or even marry a particular person simply in the hopes of pleasing their parents and winning the attention they so crave.

That's the power our parents have as the primary and most influential "well" in our lives, and the same power *we* have over the lives of our children. We empower our wells in such a way because we need something from them, whether love, affection, attention, approval, encouragement, money, whatever. Our drive for love and attention is so strong that if we are not careful, we will end up settling for personal unhappiness in our effort to make our parents happy. Anytime we place our "well's" happiness above our own, we lose our ability to choose. Rather than choosing what is best for us, we choose what we think is best for them in the belief that if we make them happy, we will finally find happiness ourselves. Unfortunately, it never works out that way.

Here's the problem: we try to *be* like our parents, *act* like our parents, and do the things that our parents want because we believe it will make them happy and cause them to love and appreciate us. More often, what happens is that they never notice at all what we are trying to do and have no idea what is going on with us. All we succeed in doing is living our life through someone else's eyes, pursuing someone else's dreams and goals for someone else's purposes. In the process, we lose sight of who we really are, or worse, never discover who we really are to start with. Sometimes this can have tragic consequences.

The film *Dead Poets Society* illustrates this in a powerful way. Set in the late 1950s, the film tells the story of John Keating, an English teacher whose free-spirited approach to teaching poetry has a profound impact on the lives of his students at an elite, strait-laced boys' preparatory academy. Calling upon them to "seize the day" (*carpe diem*), he opens their eyes to untapped creativity within themselves and possibilities they have barely dreamed of before.

In one scene, Todd Anderson and Neil Perry, two of Keating's students, are talking on an overhead walkway. Although it is Todd's birthday, he is feeling glum. His parents have sent him as a gift a nice desk set complete with blotter, pencil holder, scissors, and the like—the exact same gift they had sent him the year before. Implied is the fact that Todd's parents don't have time for him and his enrollment at the boarding school is a convenient way to deal with the situation. After acknowledging Todd's feelings, Neil remarks of the gift, "It's rather aerodynamic isn't it? I can feel it. This desk set wants to fly. Todd? The world's first unmanned flying desk set." Spurred on by his friend, Todd flings the desk set over the walkway to break apart below. Todd cries out in satisfaction, "Oh, my!" Neil says, "Well, I wouldn't worry. You'll get another one next year."

The central story in the film, however, belongs to Neil. Neil's personal dream is to become an actor but he is completely dominated by his father, who insists that Neil is going to go to Harvard and become a doctor. Mr. Perry is so forceful that Neil has never been able to stand up to him and say how he really feels. Under Mr. Keating's influence, however, Neil dares to dream of fulfilling his own desire. Behind his father's back and in defiance of his father's demands, Neil auditions for and wins the central role of "Puck" in a local production of Shakespeare's *A Midsummer Night's Dream*.

Neil's father learns of his involvement in the play and nearly pulls him out of it, even the day before the performance. In the end, he allows Neil to go ahead. Neil's performance in the play is brilliant and he comes away excited at the possibility of his future in theater. His hopes are dashed, however, when his father takes him home and tells him in no uncertain terms that he is through with "this acting business." Fearing that Neil has been corrupted by Mr. Keating's free-spirited teaching style, Mr. Perry has decided to remove Neil from the academy and enroll him in a military school. He will not allow Neil to ruin his life or waste his opportunities. Neil *will* go to Harvard and become a doctor.

Unable as always to stand up to his father, Neil simply gives in. That same night, however, while his parents are asleep, Neil enters his father's study and kills himself with his father's pistol.

> *There are people today who are still trying to live their lives through their parents' eyes.*

In some ways, Mr. Perry was over-attentive to Neil in dominating him and controlling and planning every aspect of his life. At the same time, however, he paid no attention to the most important thing of all: Neil's feelings and desires. Love was not the issue. Mr. Perry loved his son, but in his determination to fulfill his *own* dream of seeing his son become a doctor, Mr. Perry was oblivious to Neil's dreams. He simply could not see the depth of Neil's desire to be an actor. In the end, Mr. Perry never really knew who his son was.

Who Do We Think We Are?

Mr. Perry's failure to appreciate and affirm Neil's dreams and desires eventually led to Neil's suicide when he finally concluded that he would never be free to live his own life. Although this story is fictional, it reflects the truth of what happens every day in the lives of millions of children, regardless of their age. There are many people today in their 30s, 40s, 50s, and older who are still trying to live their lives through their parents' eyes, still striving to fulfill the life their parents dreamed for them, rather than following their own dream. The child inside them, ever dependent upon the attention and the approval that have never come, has never been free to pursue its own life and dreams.

What about you? Can you identify with Neil? Maybe you're thinking, *Yeah, that's me, all right. Mom never has understood me. Dad doesn't even know who I am. No matter what I say or do, it doesn't make any difference. My hopes and dreams and desires don't mean anything. All that matters is what they want.*

Let's look a little deeper. If you are a parent, ask yourself this question: *How am I responding to my own children?* Are you like Mr. Perry, desiring to live *your* dreams through the lives of your children instead of allowing them to live their own dreams? When your children come to your "well," what kind of water do they draw?

We need to ask ourselves, *Who do we think we are?* Do we realize how much power we have as parents? Do we understand that as fathers and mothers we have incredible power to make or break our children's hearts simply in the way we respond to them in being sensitive to their needs, desires, and dreams? Children need consistent discipline and firm guidance, but they also need tenderness and gentleness with plenty of encouragement and affirmation. Why do we as parents sometimes find this so hard to comprehend? Why can't we grasp the fact that when we bring a new life, a new heart, into the world, we have the power either to feed or to starve, to love or to abuse that new heart?

Some parents never make that connection. They never understand either the depth of the power they have to make or break their children's spirits or the depth of their children's need for love and affirmation. Time after time those children go to their parents' well for the emotional support they need, and time after time they leave empty-handed.

Children are great imitators; that's the way they learn. Think about it. How do children learn to walk? To talk? To go to the bathroom? To eat with a fork and spoon? To dress themselves? They learn all these things by watching their parents and imitating what they see.

Children also thrive on praise and encouragement. Most of us as parents are great during those earliest months at encouraging our children. We get so excited at their first step or their first word or when they "go potty" for the first time. Why do we so often let it stop there? Why can't we understand that our children need praise and affirmation and acceptance and approval and love and attention throughout their nurturing years (and beyond) and not just while they are learning to walk and talk?

One of the root problems many of us have as parents is our failure to understand how *absorbent* the hearts of our children are. Whatever we say to them, good or bad, in word, gesture, or expression, they soak up like a sponge. "You are so stupid!" "Can't you do anything right?" "You'll never amount to anything!" "Why can't you be good? I love you when you're good." Words such as these cut like a knife into the sensitive heart of a child. "I love you." "I'm very proud of you." "Nice try. You're learning." "Come on, let's work on this together." These are the kinds of words that feed a child's spirit.

Words have power. Whatever a child absorbs into his or her heart, positive or negative, particularly in the formative years, becomes a foundation for how that child views and responds to the world. If we grow up hearing how bad we are all the time, or how dumb or stupid we are, that is how we will see ourselves, and we will behave accordingly. Those negative words will become a self-fulfilling prophecy. The opposite is just as true. If our growing-up years are filled with messages of hope, affirmation, and encouragement, we will learn to see the world in a positive way. The positive words we hear as children will empower us to succeed and thrive in life.

Because words have power, we must be very careful what we say to our children and how we say it. This is especially true for those of us who grew up in a negative, abusive, condemning, or simply non-affirming environment. What we grow up with is what we tend to become, and what we become is what we tend to pass on to the next generation. Where will the cycle end? It has to end with us.

Whatever words a child absorbs in his or her formative years become that child's foundational view of the world.

Do you want to put your children through what you went through? When they draw from your well, what will their hearts absorb? Just because your past may be full of empty wells does not mean that your well has to be empty for them. Regardless of your personal experience, you can change the environment for your children. But it may not be easy.

Why Is It So Hard to Love?

Why do so many of us find it so hard to love? What's the big deal? Is it because of the empty wells in our past? Do we have trouble loving because we have never felt loved? Do we find it hard to express approval or appreciation because we

have never experienced either one? Is showing love and affirmation difficult for us because we never had a decent model?

Our ability to express our love has a lot to do with how we
saw love modeled by our parents and other significant adults
in our lives when we were children. In most cases, love itself
was not the issue, but the effectiveness of its expression.
Silent love or love without action is hard to distinguish from
indifference, particularly for children. Some parents, emotionally starved themselves while growing up, ply their kids with
money and material things in an effort to prove their love
because that is all they know to do. As children, they did
everything they could and gave everything they could to get
love from an empty well in their lives. Even though it didn't
work, they still do the same thing today—they give, give, give
to get, get, get—because they don't know any other way.

Material possessions are a poor substitute for love, and children know the difference in their hearts even if they can't articu-
late it in their minds. All they know is that they hurt inside with a
nagging ache that won't go away and that they cannot identify.

What are we doing to our children? How hard is it to say,
"I love you" or "I'm proud of you"? How difficult is it to give a
word of praise or encouragement every now and then? Why is
it that so many of our children hear nothing but criticism from
our lips? Do we have any idea of the pain we have brought
and are bringing on our children by our inability or our unwill-
ingness to show our love in truly meaningful ways?

Sad to say, sometimes it takes a tragedy to shock us into
an awareness of what could have been. One of life's ironies is
that so often the nicest things ever said about a person are
said at the funeral. Why do we have to wait until someone dies

to cry? Why do have to wait until someone dies to tell how we really feel? Why do we put it off and put it off and put it off until all we have left is regrets?

Sometimes the hardest thing in the world is to overcome the "programming" of our childhood. As children we learned to relate to the world by imitating the words, attitudes, and behavior of our parents or guardians. Over time, we internalized that imitation until it became our own, our way of life. The big problem with imitation, however, is its artificiality. Imitation is important as a starting place, a stepping stone, but healthy development means adding to that model our own individuality and uniqueness. As long as all we do is imitate someone else, we will never come to know and be ourselves.

Through imitation, we tend to become like those whose model we see, whether good or bad. Think about it. Do you *really* want to be like your mother or your father? Depending on the model they gave you, maybe you do. If your parents were for you a well that was continually full of love and affirmation and acceptance and approval, and a refuge of stability and consistency in discipline and behavior, you may feel that the best thing you can possibly do is to emulate them.

On the other hand, maybe you don't. Looking back on your childhood may bring up very different memories of your parents: rejection, emotional coldness, inconsistent discipline, unpredictable behavior, lack of approval or acceptance, too caught up in their own problems to notice yours. Maybe you have decided that the last thing in the world you want is to be like them. This doesn't mean that you reject your parents or that you no longer love them. It simply means that you realize that you need to look elsewhere for the emotional fulfillment and the model you need.

This raises some additional questions. Take a hard, honest look at yourself. What model are you giving to your children? What kind of legacy of love and affirmation are you leaving for them? It doesn't matter how old they are.

Do you really want your children to be like you?

Whenever they are around you, do they have to beg for your attention? Are they reaching out desperately to you for even one crumb of encouragement, one scrap of approval, or even the tiniest inkling that you know and appreciate them for who they are? The example you set now may affect your descendants for generations to come. As you are right now, do you *really* want your children to be like you?

Modeling God

More is at stake here than just the emotional health and well-being of our children and ourselves. There is also a spiritual dimension to consider. Right or wrong, the way we act toward our children will teach them to perceive and think about God in a particular way. If our children have to beg for *our* attention, they will grow up believing they have to beg for *God's* attention as well. If they have trouble believing that *we*, their fathers or mothers, love them, they will have trouble believing that *God*, their heavenly Father, loves them.

Emotionally dehydrated, love-starved people often grow up to be obsessed with achievement. Because their natural thirst for love, affirmation, and approval has never been satisfied, they push and push and push and work and work and work day after day after day trying to please a parent or a spouse or a boss or a pastor. Their underlying motivation, usually unspoken and often not fully understood even by themselves is, *If I do a little more, he will love me,* or *If I work just a little harder, she will approve of me,* or *If I work some more voluntary overtime, my boss will notice.*

Because this has become the pattern of their lives and thought, they will act the same way toward God. They will do more and work harder than others around them in the hopes of catching God's attention and winning His acceptance and approval. This is the way millions of people around the world approach God. They assume that God (however they perceive Him) is a distant, aloof entity with little involvement and even less interest in the affairs of individual people. To get His attention, they feel they have to pray more, do more, work more, make more sacrifices, and give more offerings than someone else. God must be persuaded, cajoled, or bribed into listening to them and doing what they want. The idea of a God who loves them simply for who they are is completely foreign to them.

Unfortunately, many people who profess to know Christ have a similar attitude. They have built their entire spiritual lives around what they think they must *do* to overcome God's reluctance and aloofness and *win* His love and acceptance. The sad part of this is that there is nothing they—or any of us—can do to win God's love. The beautiful part is that we don't have to; *we already have God's love!* God loves us because He created us. He loves us because He is God and is by nature love. God's love is unconditional; it does not depend on what we do or do not do. We do not have to beg for God's attention. He is intimately interested in every one of us and pursues a relationship with each of us with a love that simply won't quit.

Here is just a sampling of what the Bible says about God and His love for us:

I have loved you with an everlasting love; I have drawn you with loving-kindness (Jeremiah 31:3b).

But you, O Lord, are a compassionate and gracious God, slow to anger, abounding in love and faithfulness (Psalm 86:15).

Give thanks to the LORD, for he is good. His love endures forever (Psalm 136:1).

For God so loved the world that he gave his one and only Son, that whoever believes in him shall not perish but have eternal life (John 3:16).

But God demonstrates his own love for us in this: While we were still sinners, Christ died for us (Romans 5:8).

For I am convinced that neither death nor life, neither angels nor demons, neither the present nor the future, nor any powers, neither height nor depth, nor anything else in all creation, will be able to separate us from the love of God that is in Christ Jesus our Lord (Romans 8:38-39).

Whoever does not love does not know God, because God is love. This is how God showed his love among us: He sent his one and only Son into the world that we might live through him. This is love: not that we loved God, but that he loved us and sent his Son as an atoning sacrifice for our sins....And so we know and rely on the love God has for us. God is love. Whoever lives in love lives in God, and God in him (1 John 4:8-10, 16).

Daddy, I'm Begging for Your Attention!

Does that sound like a God who needs to be persuaded to listen to us; to be talked into loving us? I don't think so! If you are looking for love to fill that emotional hole in your heart, turn to God. He can fill it completely. If you are looking for a model of love and acceptance to place before your children, then model God.

Don't Give Up

Maybe you're thinking, *That's all fine and good, but it's too late for me. My kids are already grown. I know I have not been the father (or mother) they needed. I know now that I never gave them the kind of love or attention or affirmation they were looking for, but what can I do about it at this late date? I don't think I can change. Besides, it probably won't do any good anyway.*

Perhaps not, but you will never know unless you try. *It is never too late to change.* The Bible says that nothing is impossible with God. Even if you have caused your children much emotional pain through the years and they have distanced themselves from you—even if you have been an "empty well" to them—it is never too late to change. The road to reconciliation may be long and hard and slow, but as long as you and they still have breath, there is hope. Don't give up.

The same thing goes for those of you who have been on the receiving end. For years you have tried to draw water from a well that was always empty, and now you are tired. You're fed up with it all. It is a hurt too deep for words. You're angry, and bitterness may be eating away at you like a cancer. You feel like you've wasted 20, 30, 40 years or more of your life looking for something you've never found. Above all, you feel

Above all, you feel deeply disappointed. You still want the relationship with your "well" that you have always craved, but fear now will never come.

Maybe it won't, but don't give up. Whether or not your "empty well" ever changes and becomes a source of healthy water for you, recovery and healing are still possible. The only one you can change is you. Your past is your past; let it stay there. Move ahead from the barrenness of unmet needs and unfulfilled dreams to the fertile valley of One who loves you with an everlasting love, One whom you never have to beg for His attention because you already have it.

Chapter Three

DO YOU EVEN SEE ME?

What would it be like to be invisible? Several years ago, the television series *The New Twilight Zone* aired an episode entitled "To See the Invisible Man." Based on a 1963 short story by Robert Silverberg, it told of a man in a futuristic society who was sentenced to one year of invisibility. His crime? Coldness toward his fellow citizens. Although he remained fully visible physically, a brand was placed on his forehead to identify him as "Invisible." This meant that by law no one could speak to him, assist him, or acknowledge his existence in any way. Anyone who did so became subject to the same sentence.

At first, the man thought his sentence of invisibility was a lark. He could go anywhere he pleased and no one would stop him. He could lift money from a cash register or steal food from a grocery store with no penalty. He could enter a movie theater or museum without paying admission. No matter where he went or what he did, no one took notice; after all, he was "invisible."

Before long, the downside of being "invisible" became evident. This man who had never before been particularly interested in other people began to hunger for human contact. He began to crave for someone to speak even one word to him. One day in a cafeteria he struck up a conversation with a blind man. Things were going well until another patron whispered the word "*Invisible*" in the blind man's ear. Muttering a curse at the invisible man for taking advantage of his blindness, the blind man moved to another table.

While crossing the street one day, the man was struck by a passing car. Because he was "invisible," no one would help him. He managed to get home on his own, but when he called the doctor on the videophone, the doctor took one look at his invisibility brand and hung up without a word.

By this time, the man had come to realize how much of a curse his invisibility was. On one occasion he encountered another "Invisible" on the street, but when he begged for attention and conversation, the other "Invisible" ignored him and ran off. In this society, even the "Invisibles" were forbidden to acknowledge each other under penalty of having their sentences extended.

Finally, the year was over and the same men who had fixed the brand on his head came to his apartment and removed it. For the first time in a year, he heard words spoken directly to him. They invited him out for a customary drink. When he hesitated, they hinted that he was being antisocial. Fearing a new sentence, he went with them.

What joy! What relief! He was visible again and fully restored to society. No longer a cold and aloof person, he had learned his lesson well—perhaps too well. One day on the street he saw a woman who bore the invisibility brand on her forehead. She was screaming and crying and begging for someone to notice her, to acknowledge her. As she caught his eye, she turned her appeal to him. At first, he started to ignore her and pass her by; after all, she was "invisible." Her continued cries, as well as the memories of his own experience as an "Invisible," stirred compassion in his heart. He reached out and embraced her, saying as she collapsed sobbing into his arms, "It's all right. I *do* see you. I *do* see you."

As he held her, hovering surveillance spheres gathered, visually recording this "crime" and warning him to step away. He ignored them. He had spent a year "invisible" for the crime of coldness. What would be his sentence for the crime of warmth?

Invisible People

Invisibility is not all it's cracked up to be. Oh, sure, it might be fun to be able to go anywhere or do anything you please any time you want with no restrictions—for a while. But what about that inevitable time when you become hungry for human contact and interaction; when you crave a simple word or a simple touch from another person? How can someone talk to you if he doesn't see you? How can he touch you if he doesn't know you are there?

Which of us has not at one time or another felt like we were invisible? At social gatherings people talk about you or around you as if you are not even in the room. In gym class in school you are always the last to be chosen for a team. In the workplace, colleagues get recognition, bonuses, and even promotions while your contributions to the company go unnoticed and unrewarded. You try to talk to someone face-to-face, but his eyes—and his attention—are focused elsewhere. Even worse, his eyes appear to look not *at* you but *through* you, as though you aren't even there. At home, you work hard to do the right thing and try to make everybody happy, but no one notices. Mom doesn't appreciate you. Dad does not recognize the sacrifices you've made. Your spouse is insensitive to what you do in the home. Your kids—well, kids are kids and often don't notice all the things you do for them.

We are not meant to be alone.

All your life you have been working, striving, laboring to please, hoping for even the tiniest bit of recognition. For years you have been begging for attention, for some scrap of acknowledgment from the primary "well" in your life, to reassure you that you matter. All to no avail. Haven't you ever felt like screaming, "Do you even see me? Do you even know I exist? I'm right here! What's the matter with you?"

Being ignored hurts so much because we are not meant to be alone. Invisibility doesn't suit us. By design and nature, we humans are social creatures. We need contact with each other. That is why we gather together in communities—in towns, villages, and cities. The poet John Donne wrote, "No man is an island, entire of itself; every man is a piece of the continent, a part of the main." Some people get by okay as hermits or loners, but not many.

In the early days of American westward expansion, it was common for pioneer families to stake out a claim in the wilderness or on the prairie and build their homestead right in the middle of it, often miles from their nearest neighbor. That way they could enjoy the peace and quiet and seclusion of their new home away from the bustle of crowded cities. It wasn't long, however, before the problems with this arrangement became evident. First of all, if they were threatened by wild animals or attacked by hostile Indians, they were on their own. No one else was near enough to render assistance.

Secondly, and just as serious, was the mental and emotional toll of loneliness. Many of these people became very eccentric, developed bizarre personality traits, and occasionally even went mad from the effects of endless bleak days of unbroken isolation. Gradually, settlers owning adjacent tracts of land learned to build their houses at adjoining corners of their property so they could benefit from mutual support, defense, and companionship.

If being ignored eats away at you inside, you're not alone. No one likes to go unnoticed. We are not built that way. From the very beginning, we were meant for love and companionship. According to the book of Genesis, after God created Adam He determined that it was not good for the man to be alone, so He made a woman to be the man's helper, companion, friend, and mate. That has been the pattern ever since. We are at our most human when we are together, loving each other, acknowledging each other, and paying attention to one another.

In this sense the world is a very inhuman place because it is full of invisible people. They are found in every culture, every society, and every nation on earth. We pass by them every day and don't even notice: the poor, the homeless, the sick, the weak, the powerless, the dirty, the ugly, the unlovable, the disenfranchised, the marginalized. Some societies, such as India, have invisibility built into their class structure.

India's "invisibles" are strictly relegated to the lowest class, or *caste*, commonly known as the "untouchables." Many of these people are born, live their entire lives, and die on the streets of India's teeming cities. The late Mother Teresa devoted her life and ministry to seeing and touching and caring for the invisible people of India.

Some of you might say, "Wait a minute; I see those people every day. I see the poor and the homeless, the sick and the dirty. They are everywhere. How could I miss them?" Of course we see them in the sense of perceiving visually that they are there. We may even notice their condition. But how often do we really *see* them for who they are: people of worth and deserving of love and dignity and respect, with hopes and dreams and needs and desires and pains and passions as real as our own? All too frequently we don't because our minds are not trained nor our hearts tuned to see them.

Invisibility is no respecter of race, religion, or social or economic status. Neither wealth nor education provide immunity. Invisible people are not limited only to inner city slums, rural backwoods, Third-World countries, or any of the other "typical" places that we think of. They go to our schools, work in our factories and offices, and attend our churches, mosques, and synagogues. They are as close as just across the street or right next door. Some may even reside under our own roof.

Emotional Non-Persons

Is there an invisible person living in your house? How would you know? It could be your son or your daughter. Parents often don't know their own children. They cannot describe their dreams, their goals, or their aspirations. They don't know what their children are good at of passionate about. Oftentimes parents don't see them—really see them—for who they are; instead, their children are only agents for carrying out the parents' agenda and fulfilling their dreams and desires. Their children—whatever their age—may not be free people in their own right but merely slaves to the parents' will. The children have to clamor for the parents to notice them or behave "right" in order to get approved.

Parents, by your own actions and attitude, have you made your children invisible? When was the last time you had a heart-to-heart talke with your kids about what they want in life? Have they become emotional non-persons?

It could be your spouse. In some marriages one spouse, usu-ally the wife (but not always), is treated by the other as little more than an overgrown child. Her opinions are disregarded, her feel-ings dismissed, her needs ignored, all in the interest of toeing the line for her husband's desires and demands. He has little regard for her intellect, ideas, or talents. She has few rights of her own. When she needs or wants money, she has to meekly ask her hus-band for it like a child begging for her allowance. She is con-stantly under her husband's thumb, totally dominated by him. Instead of being his companion and helper, she has become his slave. The person she truly is, a person of value, worth, gifted-ness, and high potential, has been completely suppressed.

Does this describe *your* marriage? Have you caused your spouse to become "invisible"? Has he or she become an emo-tional non-person?

It could be your mother or your father. Sometimes the tables are turned and parents become invisible to their chil-dren. This is quite common in situations where the children grew up invisible to their parents. One of the laws of human life is that we tend to reproduce ourselves in our children. In other words, our children usually turn out to be just like us. The late Harry Chapin captured this truth very poignantly in his timeless song "Cat's in the Cradle." A father regrets that he never had time for his son while the boy was growing up, and now his son, a man himself, has no time for his father. Too late the father realizes, as he laments in the last verse, "And as I hung up the phone, it occurred to me, he'd grown up just like me. My boy was just like me."[1]

Rarely do children deliberately make their parents invisible. There is no retaliation involved; they merely act according to the example they were taught. When parents have no time for their children, their children learn to seek their emotional fulfillment elsewhere, and that transfers into adulthood. Why return to the original "well" that in the past always turned up empty?

Nevertheless, parents who feel invisible to their children experience pain just as real as that of children who are ignored by their parents. Related to this, a woman named Muriel[2] shared her story with me:

> My husband passed away ten years ago. We had been married for many years and his loss was devastating to me. Part of my family gathered around me and watched over me, but my son, who is a very successful businessman, seemed oblivious to the needs of the rest of the family. It seemed that each time I would try to reach out to him he would say something to hurt me. As a result, I have stopped trying to see him very often. I thought that we would still be a family even though the father is now gone, but it is not so. Even though ours seems to be a dysfunctional family, we are all trying to

be normal. I have three wonderful grandchildren who are so good to me, and we love to be together.

This week I had the opportunity at the airport to view a family reunion. The mother was just getting off the plane and the father and children rushed to hug her and she was weeping with joy to see them. They had waited so eagerly, hoping she would get there soon. To me, that's what a family is.

Each time I try to reach out to my son he says by his actions, "I'm too busy for you." I say to myself, "Well, you were a poor mother and you deserve this." But then I think, "Well, you're not the best, but you tried."

He has been very successful, though, and I am thankful for that.

Can't you feel in Muriel's words the pain that is in her heart? The pain of losing her husband? The regret over her "dysfunctional" family? The sting of rejection in her rebuffed efforts to reach out to her son? Her guilt in the feeling that it may be her fault? The bittersweet tang of maternal love and pride in a successful son who seems to have no time for her; a son to whom she has become invisible?

What about you? Have you become so emotionally distant from your parents that they have become invisible to you? Have you made them emotional non-persons?

Perhaps the invisible person in your house is *you*. No matter what you do, no one seems to notice. As far as your spouse or your children or your parents are concerned, your feelings don't matter. Your dreams and desires don't matter. Your ideas and opinions don't matter. Your achievements and accomplishments don't matter. For all the difference you make, you might as well not even be there. Time after time and year after year you have gone to the well looking for a drink only to go away still thirsty and hurting more than you did when you came. The child inside you knows you should feel love, but where is it? You know you should find encouragement and emotional support and affirmation and acceptance at home, but where are they? It seems as though nobody cares about you or who you really are. In fact, most of the time they act as though they can't even see you. What's worse, if they do see you, then obviously they are ignoring you. You have become invisible. Emotionally, you have become a non-person.

> *One of the worst things we can do to a person is ignore him.*

Acting Out

One of the worst things we can do to another person is to ignore him. The "silent treatment" is just as cruel and painful emotionally as the so-called Chinese water torture, where water drips incessantly onto a person's forehead one drop at a time as he slowly goes insane. As cruel as it is, however, sometimes we are quick to use the silent treatment because it is an effective weapon in controlling others. We use it to punish someone. Has anyone ever ignored you to let you know he was angry or displeased? We use it to encourage conformity by ignoring non-conforming behavior and rewarding conforming behavior. Have you ever ignored your child because he or she did not do what you wanted the way you wanted it done?

How can we be so cruel, so unfeeling, so insensitive to the tender, moldable, and easily crushable hearts of our children?

Children who are ignored act out in different ways in order to be noticed. The more they are ignored, the more drastic their acting out will become. Left unsatisfied, ignored children who act out will grow into adults who act out. Although the methods they employ may change, their motivation is the same: to get attention. The crybaby, temper-tantrum-in-the-grocery-store type of acting out may give way to more dangerous and self-destructive behavior such as violence, general lawlessness, and substance abuse. The prisons of America are filled with such people.

Sometimes children obsessed with being seen become adults obsessed with job performance or with gathering wealth or influence or power. They are so starved for attention that their whole life becomes a campaign to be *seen*—to make themselves known and noticed by others. Invisible and ignored by the person or persons they need recognition from the most, they try to compensate by making themselves highly visible in other areas to other people.

Ah, Look at All the Lonely People

One direct consequence of invisibility is loneliness. Let's face it, invisible people are lonely people. If you have ever felt invisible, you know it's true. It doesn't matter how many people may be around you, feeling invisible is a very lonely feeling. Invisibility isolates us, separates us, cuts us off emotionally from those around us. That is why it is possible to be lonely in the middle of a large crowd.

There is a difference between being *lonely* and being *alone*. Aloneness is a state of being; loneliness is a state of mind. You can be completely alone and yet not feel lonely when you are secure and confident in the love and affirmation of other people even when they are not present. In other words, a positive emotional connection with another person is a strong inoculation against loneliness.

Lonely people lack such an emotional connection. Somewhere along the way their relational cord has been severed, leaving them with no close relationships, no one to call a friend, no one to turn to for encouragement or support, no one who seems to care whether they live or die. They have no source for quenching their emotional thirst. All they have is the sense-deadening prospect of endless bleak days of wandering in a world where no one ever sees them or takes notice of them or even knows they are alive. They are like Eleanor Rigby in the classic Beatles' song:

> *Eleanor Rigby picks up the rice in the church where a wedding has been*
>
> *Lives in a dream.*
>
> *Waits at the window, wearing a face that she keeps in a jar by the door*
>
> *Who is it for?*
>
> *...Eleanor Rigby died in the church and was buried along with her name*
>
> *Nobody came...*
>
> *(Chorus)*
>
> *All the lonely people*

Do You Even See Me?

Where do they all come from?

All the lonely people

Where do they all belong?[3]

Who are the "Eleanor Rigbys" in your life? Are there lonely people right under your nose? Someone who calls you "Boss"? Someone who calls you "Teacher"? Someone who eats at your table? Someone who shares your bed? Someone who calls you "Daddy" or "Mommy"?

Take a good look at yourself. No matter who you are, someone depends on you for emotional support, for love and acceptance, for validation that has meaning and value. What does this person receive when he or she comes to you? Is he or she able to be filled with full, refreshing draughts of water from an abundant supply, or do you by your actions and attitude condemn him or her to a barren desert of parching thirst, crushing loneliness, and spirit-withering invisibility?

Seeing Into the Soul

What does it take to see invisible people? Obviously, it requires a whole new way of looking at things. Somehow we have to get beyond our skim-the-surface philosophy and learn how to plumb the depths of the greater realities that lie beneath. Ours is a very superficial, self-centered, and self-seeking world that has no mercy on the weak or the sensitive and is quick to lacerate the unwary. Consequently, most of us learn at a very early age to hide our true feelings under a cloak of superficial and inconsequential chatter and to disguise our true selves under a mask of either confidence or indifference.

Nobody likes to be hurt, so we submerge our true selves, that child within us, deep below the surface in order to protect it. Many of us refuse to take a close look inside because we are afraid of what we might find there. We fear that we may not like the person we see inside. For the same reason, we refuse to let anyone else get too close to us. If they do, and if they get a good look at us, they may not like us either.

We can only begin to see the invisible people around us by learning to let our guard down.

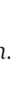

It is dangerous to really look at another person and see that person for who he or she really is because in the process we make ourselves vulnerable and open to the same scrutiny. We can't see into another person's life without opening up our own, and that thought scares a lot of people. Think about it. Are you ready or willing to let someone else see who you really are with no facades, no masks, no disguises, and no defenses? So many of us have been hurt so many times that our defenses are always in place; we always have our guard up. When someone starts to get too close to the raw emotional core of our beings, we close up and retreat into ourselves.

The only way we can begin to see the invisible people in our lives is by learning to let our guard down. We do not see them because we choose not to see them. Seeing is risky. Seeing means letting them approach us, which might allow them to see more of us than we want them to see. They might touch that rawness in our spirits and stir up our pain all over again. Our carefully laid façade of a life in control might suddenly collapse like a house of cards.

Do You Even See Me?

Invisible people become visible again when we take the time to look deep into their souls, but we have to be willing at the same time to let them look deep into ours. Are you ready for that? Can you stand up to the scrutiny of someone else's eyes probing deep into your life?

The eyes are the windows of the soul. If you know how to look, you can gaze into someone's eyes and see right into his heart, and he can do the same with you. This doesn't happen often because few of us have the confidence and self-assurance to make ourselves that vulnerable. Our shallow society has conditioned us to "see" only on a superficial level. Most of us glide through life simply skimming the surface, rarely probing any deeper. Seeing on the surface only, however, often leads to a distorted view because few things in life are as they appear to be. It is only when we develop "X-ray vision" of a sort and dig beneath the surface that we come to see and understand the truth. British poet William Blake wrote:

> This life's dim windows of the soul
>
> Distorts the heavens from pole to pole
>
> And leads you to believe a lie
>
> When you see with, not through, the eye.

How do you view the world? Do you see it simply *with* your eyes, skimming the surface, taking what you see at face value but never engaging your heart? Or do you view it *through* your eyes, letting the passion and perceptions of your heart help you shape and understand what you see? That which is inside us inevitably influences how we view the world. If you have a lot of garbage in your soul, then the world will appear to you like one huge trash dump. If your soul is full of joy and good memories and beautiful things, then the world will be like a garden for you. Most of us fall somewhere in between.

This is what Jesus was referring to when He said:

Your eye is the lamp of your body. When your eyes are good, your whole body also is full of light. But when they are bad, your body also is full of darkness. See to it, then, that the light within you is not darkness. Therefore, if your whole body is full of light, and no part of it dark, it will be completely lighted, as when the light of a lamp shines on you (Luke 11:34-36).

What is inside us influences how we view the world.

Every piece of garbage that enters our lives dims our ability to see. Every rejection, every harsh word, every cutting criticism, every time we are ignored, every time we are made to feel invisible, every time we draw from our well and come up empty; each of these darkens the glass a little more, clouding our vision. It is no wonder, then, that the empty well syndrome tends to be self-perpetuating. If our own vision is so distorted by the cumulative effects of the empty well in our own lives, how can we possibly see clearly enough to avoid doing the same to our own children?

The Choice Is Ours

We must *choose* to see clearly. We must choose to apply emotional and spiritual Windex to the glass and clean away the dirt and the smudges and the darkness. We must choose to no longer allow the garbage, the hurts, and the disappointments of our past to stand in the way of our seeing clearly. We must choose to look another person in the eye and allow him or her to do the same. Something deep, something intense, something spiritual happens when we look at others this way.

When you take the time and the risk to really look into the eyes of someone for whom you are a well, you will see the desire, the longing, and the hope he or she harbors in the heart. You will see the untapped potential inside this person, waiting to be released. You will come to understand the power you have—simply by how you respond—to either feed or starve this heart, to either fill or deny its desires and longings, to either build up or crush its hopes, and to either liberate or suppress its potential.

No matter how things may have been in the past, learning to look at someone this way can begin to build a certain level of love in you that makes you want to be who that person needs you to be, and provide what that person needs you to provide, even if you feel you are not yet equipped to do it. Sometimes the difference between success and failure, between being a full well or an empty well, hinges on the way we see another person and how we respond to what we see.

When my wife and I first learned that she was pregnant with our daughter, we were overjoyed and ecstatic! We were going to have our first child! But then lying in bed awake one night not long after, it suddenly hit me: I was going to be a father! *A father!* As the magnitude of that reality began to sink in, my head began to buzz with all sorts of thoughts and questions. What kind of father would I be? I have a youth ministry with around 700 young people, 80 percent of whom have no father in the home. In my counseling sessions I have heard countless stories of abusive fathers, absentee fathers, incestuous fathers, drunkard fathers, drug-wasted fathers—you name it. *God,* I prayed, *don't let me mess this up.* Then I thought, What kind of father did I *want* to be to my daughter?

Did I want to be a "Cat's in the Cradle" kind of father, too busy for his child until it was too late? Did I want my daughter to grow up uncertain of my love and so starved for attention that she would act out in increasingly unhealthy ways? Did I want to raise her to be lonely or to feel invisible around me? Did I want to be an empty well for her, with no emotional sustenance to give her when she came to me? Did I want her to grow up with emotional pain and cravings I could not satisfy? *Absolutely not!*

Did I want her to grow up happy, fulfilled, and well-adjusted, ready to move confidently into the world? Did I want her to be able to look at me and feel safe, loved, and affirmed? Did I want her to know she was the most special and precious person in the world to me? Did I want to be able to look deep into her eyes and see not fear but love and joy and peace and security? Did I really want to see my daughter go beyond my abilities and opportunities, to prosper more than me, and to move higher in social status? Did I want to see her succeed in every possible way? *Absolutely!*

When I was in the early stages of working on this book and was thinking about this whole idea of the way we see other people, a friend of mine suggested that I take a deep look into my daughter's eyes and note what I saw. My daughter is now a year and a half old. When I looked into her precious, trusting, loving eyes, I saw that she had such tremendous potential and that she was depending 100 percent on me. That left me with a choice to make. I could either live as an empty well and offer nothing to her—potentially affecting her future children—or I could choose to make a difference, get filled up, and become a full well for her.

As I pondered these things, out of my heart came the conviction that I wanted, more than anything, to be a well of life for my daughter. In fact, with all my heart I determined to be an abundant well of love and affirmation for my wife, too. I want to do everything I can to make sure that whenever they come to me they will find an abundant supply of fresh water to slake their thirst and rejuvenate their spirits.

One Saturday while I was working on my message for Sunday, my daughter wanted to go for a walk. She was pulling at me and tugging on my arm trying to get my attention. Finally, when I didn't respond quickly enough for her, she hit me! One of the things we are teaching our daughter is not to hit. Every parent goes through that with a child. Now, I had to stop right then and there and ask myself, "Am I going to yell at this baby or discipline her for hitting me simply because she wanted my attention?" I chose not to discipline her because I realized that she was simply trying to get me to notice her so we could go for a walk. What else could I do? I put my stuff down, grabbed her coat, and we went to the park and played for three hours. What a joy it was to watch her run and play, to listen to her giggles of delight, and to see the pure joy on her face and the love in her eyes as she spent time with her "Daddy!" There is no feeling in all the world quite like it!

That's how you make a difference. That's how you break the cycle. Learn to recognize the behavior of those who are after your attention. Develop the ability to see the invisible people who are looking to you for filling, and then act on what you see and give them what they need. It is not automatic. Change comes only by choice. Becoming a full well of life for those under our influence, whether at home, or at work, or anywhere else, is a decision each of us must make. Otherwise, it won't happen.

Endnotes

1. Harry Chapin, "Cat's in the Cradle." Album: *Verities and Balderdash.* 1974

2. Not her real name.

3. Lennon/McCartney, "Eleanor Rigby." Album: *Revolver.* 1966.

Part Two:

TURNING POINT—
SELF-DISCOVERY

Chapter Four

MY WELL IS EMPTY

Four days into the desert, his water ran out. The empty canteen hung uselessly around his neck as he stumbled across the parched, cracked ground, the blazing sun leeching moisture from his body with his every step. Far behind him his Jeep, its engine burned out, sat inert and lifeless in the sand. Ahead of him—if his map was correct—lay an old mining property where he hoped to find shelter—and water.

By the sixth day, too weak to walk, he was crawling on his hands and knees. There was nothing around him but sun, sand, and sparse, scrubby brush, a panorama unbroken in every direction as far as his eyes could see. His tongue, dry and swollen, was like a wad of cotton in his mouth. His sun-blistered skin had already begun to peel, and the chapped and cracked cuts on his knuckles no longer oozed blood. He was too dry to bleed.

Suddenly, up ahead, what was that? A glint of light, a reflection of—water? New energy surged into his body as he rose to a crouch and half crawled, half ran toward the image glimmering in the heat rising from the arid ground. No matter how far he ran, however, he never seemed to get any closer. It remained tauntingly out of reach. So focused was he on his goal that he never saw the ground drop away. Tumbling forward, he landed hard at the bottom of a dry streambed. Climbing painfully up the other side, he looked around, but the image was gone. No water. Only a mirage; nothing more.

Increasingly desperate, he forced himself forward on hands and knees, but his weakening body did not want to cooperate. His arms and legs kept giving out underneath him. It was all he could do to keep moving. After what seemed like hours of crawling, his ears caught the faint rasp of metal against metal, very close. By now, he was practically blind from the sun's glare. Squinting his eyes, he was able to make out a fence with a broken down metal gate hanging on one hinge, moving slightly in the gentle breeze. A sign on the gate said, "Abbott Mining Company. Keep Out." A short distance beyond the gate he saw a tiny shack with one wall and part of the roof collapsed. Next to the shack was—a well!

Gathering all the strength he could muster, he scrambled through the gap in the hanging gate. He pulled himself forward until he collapsed against the stone wall of the well. From the position of the rope, he could tell that the bucket was already at the bottom. Propping himself against the well's wall, he grasped the wooden crank with both hands and began to turn it. He felt the weight of the bucket as it began to rise. It was heavy! That must mean water! Licking his cracked lips with his swollen tongue, he could already almost taste the water he would soon enjoy. It seemed an eternity before the bucket reached the top of the well. Grasping it with both hands, he turned it up over his face and was rewarded with a cascade of—sand. Sand! The well was empty!

Dropping the bucket, he slid to the ground and leaned against the wall of the well, his body wracked by tearless sobs. He was too dry for tears. As his crying subsided and he calmed down a little, he heard the soft but unmistakable sound of trickling water. Following the sound with his eyes, he spotted another small shack about a hundred yards behind the well. It looked to him like a springhouse. That shack was the source of the sound.

With a desperation that only someone in the last throes of thirst could muster, he crawled and scrambled toward the shack. The sound of water got louder as he approached. A weather-beaten sign outside the springhouse read, "Warning! This spring has been contaminated by chemical pollutants and is unsafe to drink. For drinking purposes, draw water from the well. Abbott Mining Company."

Ignoring the warning, he pushed his way through the door of the springhouse. Water bubbled up from the spring into a small, stone-lined pool. Dropping to his stomach, he plunged his cupped hands into the cool water, brought them up to his face, and drank draught after draught.

Looking for Love in All the Wrong Places

People who are thirsty enough will do anything necessary to satisfy their thirst, even if it means drinking contaminated or poisonous water. If you are desperately thirsty, the *risk* of sickness from drinking bad water is preferable to the *certainty* of death by dehydration, especially if you have no other option. Thirst overrides every other consideration. When you need water, suddenly nothing else seems important.

When you need water, nothing else is important.

It is the same way with people who are thirsty for love and affirmation. That thirst will outweigh every other priority, and they will devote all their time, effort, and resources to satisfying it. Depending on how desperate they are, their thirst for love may drive them to do drastic or foolish things. They may enter into a bad relationship just because it makes them feel good for a while. They may start to abuse drugs or alcohol as a way of deadening their pain and substituting a chemical "high" for the love that is missing in their lives. They may adopt a high-risk lifestyle, seeking increasingly dangerous thrills to compensate for the emotional deadness in their hearts. Self-destructive behavior may also be a response to a love-parched soul.

We all have a love-shaped hole in our hearts, and if love is absent, we *will* find *something* to fill that hole. Our thirst for love often makes us willing to sacrifice anything—our time, our dignity, even our self-respect—in order to satisfy it. If the primary "well" in our lives cannot or will not supply what we need, we will turn elsewhere, even if it means looking for love in all the wrong places.

Have You Tested Your Well Lately?

Anyone who has a well as the primary water supply for their home knows that the water must be tested periodically to ensure that it is safe to drink. Groundwater can be contaminated in many different ways. Routine testing and treatment of well water for hardness, salinity, presence of lead or other harmful elements or minerals and bacteria or other disease-causing microorganisms can help prevent sickness and other water-related problems. People who ignore these precautions and simply go to the well time after time assuming everything will always be okay are only fooling themselves. Eventually, they will get themselves in trouble.

When was the last time you tested your well? I'm not talking about a literal water well, but the person who is the primary emotional well in your life, the one you turn to most to draw the love, affirmation, acceptance, and support you need. When you draw from your well, what quality of water do you get from it?

We all have people we depend on for guiding us on our journey through life. These people are like wells whose water we draw from when we are thirsty. This water is the love, affirmation, approval, encouragement, knowledge, wisdom, counsel, and support that we all need to become successful, well-nourished, and well-adjusted people. Life can be brutal at times, leaving us bruised and hurting, discouraged, disappointed, and despondent, drained of energy and confidence. How refreshing it is to be able to go back to our well and receive the emotional, moral, and spiritual encouragement we need to keep going!

What happens if your well is empty? What do you do if you drop your bucket into your well expecting water but instead draw up nothing but sand? How then do you meet that need in your life? How do you fill the love-shaped hole in your heart? Where do you find the emotional nourishment and support you need? How long do you keep going back to a well that does not give you what you are searching for?

One of the saddest things in life is watching people return time and again to the same empty well and always leave with the same empty result. Day after day, month after month, year after year, they go back to the same source hoping against hope to find that which will quench their thirst. One definition of insanity is doing the same thing over and over and expecting different results. Many people waste many resources and many years of their lives in the insane pursuit of water from a well that will never produce what they need. How long must such a cycle continue? When will the pattern be broken?

Does this describe your life? Is the need for love, affirmation, attention, and approval from the ones who mean the most to you a continuing, aching thirst that is never satisfied? Have you wasted much time and energy returning repeatedly to a well that no longer has what you need? Are you beginning to suspect that it never did?

At some point you have to come to the realization, "My well is empty."

When the Door Finally Slams Shut

People react to pain differently. Some have a low tolerance for pain while others can endure tremendous pain before seeking relief. Severe or ongoing pain has a way of sharpening our focus. At some point, depending on our pain threshold, it drives us to look for healing.

There was a dog that had a favorite spot on a gigantic porch. Although he could have lain anywhere on the porch, his preferred spot was at the edge right next to the steps leading down to the lush, green lawn. Over the years, the dog really settled into his spot on the porch, even wearing away in the wood a special groove that fit only him. After a while, he began to notice that every time he went to his favorite spot and lay down, his side would start to hurt. He wondered about this but, being a dog, didn't waste much time with it.

Day after day, month after month, year after year, he always lay in his special spot, even though the pain continued and grew worse. Finally, the pain got so bad that his side became infected and he required surgery and medication to heal it. Gradually over time, the wearing of the wood had exposed the sharp end of a nail. Every time the dog lay down in that spot, the nail would rub against his side, break the skin, and cause a small bleeding wound. Before the wound had a chance to scab over and heal properly, the dog would return to his spot and reopen the wound. In the end, the whole thing could have been avoided if the dog had only chosen a new spot on the porch. Instead, he had insisted on returning to the place of his pain until the pain got so bad that he was forced to do something about it.

The empty well syndrome is like that. Sometimes we don't even realize what is happening around us. We have pain, and we may even understand the source of our pain, but because we are comfortable where we are, we cover the pain and pretend that it does not exist. It is only when we lie down in that specially carved-out place that we think is going to make us happy that the nail pokes us to remind us that this is no longer working. The signs are all around us but we fail to recognize them because we think that our answer, our miracle, the thing that we have longed for, is in that place. Sometimes the pain has to become unbearable before our focus sharpens enough to see that a change is needed. Sometimes an emotional door has to slam shut to make us understand that our well is empty.

> *Sometimes the pain has to become unbearable before we see the need for change.*

The day comes when we finally realize that the thing we needed so badly that we were willing to put up with the pain—the thing we were convinced would kill us if we didn't get it—in fact does not kill us. Instead, it wakes us up to the fact that for the first time in our lives we are free from that which has haunted us for so many years. With that freedom, a door shuts almost magically on our pain and it starts to turn into healing. We know we are healed when, even though the memory of the hurt may remain, the pain is gone. Proof of healing is when we can freely make the choice to go somewhere else rather than return to our special groove with its painful nail.

One evening a buddy of mine named John came up to me and said he needed to talk. A little later, over a cup of coffee at Starbuck's, he poured out his story. John and his two brothers work with their father in the corporate world. Their father is very successful and well-respected in his field. It wasn't always that way. As John tells it:

> Our parents divorced when we were all very young. Suddenly, Dad was thrust into the situation of trying to raise three little boys on his own while building a business at the same time. Let me tell you, Dad was a real

trooper. He took care of us, provided for our needs, and made sure we always had plenty of food to eat and decent clothes to wear. He was never an absentee father, but always there when we needed him.

As I grew older, however, it seemed to me that Dad was more interested or more caught up in his business than he was in me. Sure, he took care of my brothers and me, but somehow I never felt quite secure in his love. It always seemed like I wanted or needed more from him emotionally than he was willing or able to give. I don't know, maybe I'm one of those people who needs more stroking than others. Anyway, I never felt satisfied emotionally. It seemed that Dad and I just could not "connect" on that level. I thought that eventually he would realize this, but he never did.

In order to get more emotional support from Dad, I began working harder, trying to find different ways to please him and to make him happy, and that performance-based activity became a lifestyle. Nothing I did ever seemed good enough for him. No matter how hard I worked, he never seemed to notice. The sacrifices I made for him went unnoticed.

Eventually, my brothers and I joined Dad in the business. As father and sons and as business associates, of course we had our disagreements, but it always came down to doing what Dad wanted. After all, he was the CEO.

Nothing, however, could ever equal the blowup he and I had a couple of months ago. It was an epiphany for me. During our regular market strategy meeting,

Dad tossed out an idea, as he often does, and floated it around the room. As usual, no one raised an objection or questioned his idea in any way—not sales, not marketing, not accounting, not advertising; nobody. Everyone on the management team respects my father. He is a powerhouse in the industry. But they also fear him. Being in the trenches every day, I hear the talk. No one dares tell him how they really feel, especially if they disagree, because they are afraid they will lose their job. They've seen it happen before.

That day, I thought Dad's idea wasn't very good—and I said so. I don't know, maybe I had a chip on my shoulder or there was something in the tone of my voice, but from the look on his face, I knew immediately that I had overstepped my bounds. After the meeting ended, I went to Dad's office to apologize. I was sincerely wrong, if not in expressing my opinion, at least in the way I had done it. I had embarrassed him and that wasn't right. In addition, I have to admit, my years of frustration and disappointment were reflected somewhat in my attitude as I tried—once again—to get Dad to see my point of view. I guess I was trying to "twist the knife" a little bit.

Almost before I knew what was happening, our meeting turned into a full-blown shouting match. Everything I tried to say he twisted and threw back at me. He threatened me with my job and went on about how unappreciative I was of everything he had done. As I stood there enduring his outburst, it suddenly dawned on me that nothing I had ever done for him made any difference at all. All my hard work, all my sacrifices, all the nights I went without sleep to get projects done, all the extra time I spent and all the extra miles I walked—he hadn't even noticed.

I had spent thirty years of my life trying to please this man, working as hard as I could to earn his attention and his approval, to merit some expression of love and appreciation from him—and for what? To realize that he was too caught up with his own affairs, the business and such, to notice my needs. Don't get me wrong; my dad overcame an abusive childhood, a failed marriage, and many other hardships and obstacles to get where he is today, and I admire and respect him for all that he has accomplished. I also love him. Nevertheless, I learned that day that, because of his own background, he was emotionally unequipped to give me what I had been seeking all my life.

At first, the pain of that realization took my breath away. It hurt so bad that I went back to my office and broke down in tears. In the end, however, the whole incident proved to be very liberating, because it opened my eyes to personal options I had never seen before. I could continue in the same vein and continue in the pain, or I could change direction and adjust my expectations. I chose to change direction.

Since that day, things have gotten better between the two of us. For the first time in my life I understand the boundaries in our relationship, and as long as I don't cross them, everything is fine. We get along well and we work well together, but an emotional door has slammed shut in my life in that direction. I know now that there are some things he cannot give me; some needs that he cannot supply, and that's okay. I am learning to look elsewhere for the emotional underpinnings of my life.

What Do You Do When Your Well Is Empty?

John is fortunate in that he discovered the reason for the emotional emptiness in his life in time to do something about it. His turning point came the day he knew for certain what he had suspected for years: the well he had turned to for emotional nurturing all his life—his father—was empty. Now he faced a choice. He could continue the pattern of the past, returning to the same empty well over and over again, ensuring himself of continued pain and frustration, or he could make a change and look for another well, a full well that would supply what he was lacking. John chose to change.

Sometimes we prefer the painful familiar to unknown change.

Making that kind of a change is not always as easy as it sounds. There is a certain psychology about people caught up in negative situations where they tend to stay there rather than seek something better. Even when we know we are in rotten circumstances, sometimes the familiar, even with its pain, seems preferable in our minds to the new and different with all of its unknowns. In addition, repeated rejection and disappointment have a way of wearing down our confidence and our initiative until we lack both the will to change and the faith to believe that we *can* change.

My Well Is Empty

Are you like John, expending all your time and energy seeking emotional support and validation from someone who is incapable of giving it? Are you frustrating yourself time and time again by trying to draw water from an empty well? How long will this cycle continue? How long will you keep returning to your empty well, even knowing that it has nothing for you? How long will it be before you decide to make a change?

John's life began to change the day he finally acknowledged fully that he had an empty well in his life and that to keep coming back to it for water was as useless and dangerous as beating his head against a brick wall. Likewise, the road to change for you begins with recognizing the empty well in your life for who he or she is and accepting the fact that you may never get from that person what you need and what you have been seeking all these years. You have to look elsewhere for those needs. You have to find a new well.

Let me be very clear here. This does *not* mean abandoning your empty well! It does not mean shutting an empty father or mother out of your life and having nothing more to do with him or her. It does not mean divorcing an empty spouse in favor of finding another one who will be a full well. Neither does it mean entering into an affair on the side to supply the emotional support you are lacking. What it does mean is learning to adjust your relationship in light of your new understanding.

Notice that when John came to recognize that his father was an empty well in his life, he did not sever his ties with his father. He simply understood and accepted the boundaries in their relationship and adjusted accordingly. Once John stopped seeking from his father what his father could not give him, their relationship improved.

Likewise, one of the first steps in your process of change is to learn and accept the boundaries and limitations of your relationship with your empty well. Stop setting yourself up for continual frustration. Don't keep asking or expecting from your empty well something that he or she cannot give you. Accept that person's limitations as well as the fact that you will have to go somewhere else to fill the needs that your empty well cannot fill for you.

Are *You* an Empty Well?

Recognizing and acknowledging the empty well in your life is the first step on a journey of self-discovery. Unlike John, many people who are drawing from empty wells never recognize the problem or, if they do, never manage to break away and find filling and healing from another well. Self-discovery begins when you realize that if you are going to find the love, affirmation, and support you have thirsted for all your life, you are going to have to take matters into your own hands.

You are going to have to take matters into your own hands.

This may not be easy for a couple of reasons. First, if you have never had that which you are searching for, you may not know where to look for it. Even if you find it, you may not know how to receive it because no one ever taught you. Second, whatever you do receive you may have trouble giving to others because, again, you were never taught how. No one modeled it for you.

My Well Is Empty

In other words, you face a double obstacle. Accepting the fact that there is an empty well in your life is one thing. Acknowledging the possibility that *you* are an empty well because of it is another. The sad fact is that people with empty wells in their lives often grow up to be empty wells themselves. Bereft of love and starved for attention yourself, you have little or none to give to anyone else or, if you do, have no idea how to express it.

Physical dehydration causes your bodily systems to start shutting down. Absent of water, your metabolism begins to prepare your body for death. In a similar manner, emotional dehydration causes the emotional side of your being to shut down. Gradually, your ability to feel or express emotions becomes deadened and insensitive. Just as physical wounds leave physical scars, emotional wounds leave emotional scars. And, like some physical scars, emotional scars can last a lifetime. Some emotional wounds never heal but remain open, festering sores that infect and contaminate your spirit and, like a contagious disease, can spread to your children and others within your sphere of influence.

Skin repeatedly torn and scarred becomes tough, calloused, and less sensitive to pain than unscarred skin. Repeated emotional scarring can lead to the desensitizing of the emotional side of our beings. As a result, we can become hard, unfeeling, and ungiving people—at least on the outside. Some of us are like French bread: hard and crusty on the outside but soft on the inside. Having been hurt so often and disappointed so many times, we have erected a tough outer shell to protect our soft inner child from any further harm. By habit we never reveal our true self or let anyone get too close to us for fear of being hurt again. If someone does happen to touch a sensitive nerve, we laugh or get angry or change the subject or walk away.

If nothing happens to change the cycle, dryness can spread throughout. Think about dried apples, bananas, and apricots, or raisins or beef jerky. What happens to these and other dehydrated or freeze-dried foods? They shrink and become hard and wrinkled, and often they are unappealing to look at. Is that the kind of person you want to be? Is that the kind of person you are, at least emotionally? Someone once said that President Calvin Coolidge, because of his dour expression and unemotional demeanor, looked as though he had been weaned on a pickle. Is that the way you would like to be remembered?

Forget for a moment the pain and hurt and disappointment because of the empty well in your life. Take a hard, honest look at yourself. Are *you* an empty well? Are there people looking to *you* for emotional support and affirmation who are going away empty-handed and more thirsty than when they came? Do you find yourself feeling angry or resentful of the demands these people in your life make on you?

What are you doing with the water in your well? Does your water flow or is it all bottled up? Has your water turned stale or become bitter? Water that does not flow anywhere becomes stagnant—stinking, dirty, and even poisonous and unhealthy for life. That is why the Dead Sea is dead. Water flows in from the Jordan River, but it has no outlet. The only way water leaves the Dead Sea is by evaporation. Because the Dead Sea has no outlet, mineral salts and other chemicals in the water have reached levels so high that no life can exist there. In like manner, whatever water you have in your well will become stagnant and poisoned unless you learn to let it flow. Then it can be a source of refreshing for you as well as others.

There are people all around you right now who need your water. The water in your well is vital to their emotional life and well-being. A person can die of physical dehydration in as little as three days. Emotional dehydration may take longer, but if it is not stopped, death is just as certain. Are the people you love dying on the vine? Have you pinched off the flow of the life-giving water of love, affirmation, and appreciation so that they are drying out like chaff ready to be blown away on the wind?

You must let your water flow in order for it to have life.

When people come to your well, they are looking for something: your approval, your love, your acceptance, your opinion, your friendship, your presence, your help, your wisdom, your kindness, or perhaps, simply *you*. You have the power to heal, to encourage, to love, to nurture, to accept, to affirm, and to enjoy every person who wants to draw from your well. You have the power to touch them in a way that no one else can. What will you give them?

Before you can give them anything, you must recognize your own need and deal with it. Self-discovery involves reaching the place where you can admit, "I am a needy person." Even though you may be grown and on your own, you still have needs that have never been satisfied. As long as you remain emotionally tied to the empty well in your life, you will be a co-dependent person. Your happiness, your joy, your sense of security and well-being will rise or fall with those of your empty well.

You will never change until you recognize the need to change.

Acknowledging that you have a problem is the most important step in moving toward recovery. You must recognize not only that you have an empty well in your life, but that your *own* well is empty also. Then and only then are you emotionally and mentally ready to do something about it. You will never change until you recognize the need to change. The choice is yours. You can break the cycle. Resolve that you will be co-dependent no more. As I did when contemplating the birth of my daughter, determine in your heart to be a full well for everyone who depends on you, and set yourself to do whatever it takes to follow through.

Change is possible. First you must recognize the problem of the empty well in your life, and then resolve to change for the better, to make a difference. But how? The answer lies in breaking the hold your empty well has on you and learning to live your own life rather than living someone else's. The answer lies in learning to take charge of your own life.

Chapter Five

GIVE ME THE REMOTE

Wouldn't it be great if life came with a remote control so you could make your life unfold the way you wanted? Just press "Play," and life would run ahead at normal speed, hour by hour and day by day. When a particularly memorable or pleasant event took place, you could say, "Oh, that was nice, let's see that again," then punch "Rewind" and play it back. You could even press "Slow" to make the experience last longer, allowing you to savor it to the fullest. The "Slow" button would also be useful in school or on other occasions when you needed extra time to understand or figure something out without getting left behind. Pressing "Pause" would allow you to reflect and ponder at your leisure, or even take a long rest, knowing that your life will wait for you. Pain or trouble coming your way? Just hit "Fast Forward" and skip past it all.

A silly dream? Of course, but it highlights the reality that we all have only one life and it runs steadily forward. Life is not like TiVo. There are no pauses, no rewinds or instant replays, no shortcuts past pain or difficulty. Since we only get one shot at life, let's make that shot count. Let's not waste it seeking water from dry and empty wells.

For people with the empty well syndrome, life is like being tied to a chair, a captive audience for viewing the program, "This Is Your Life," while someone else controls the remote. You see what *they* want you to see when *they* want you to see it, speeded up, slowed down, repeated at their will. Your life is completely under their control and at their mercy. It is like the beginning of the old 1960s TV series, *The Outer Limits*, where the TV screen goes through a lot of different visual effects while a somber voice intones, "We control the vertical...we control the horizontal...for the next hour we will control everything you see and hear."

No matter what else you do, as long as you allow your empty well to control your life, you will never be truly free. It's time to break the ropes and get off of that chair. It's time to take control of your life again, to take control of the remote.

Out of Control?

Although it may have taken a long time, you have finally recognized that there is an empty well in your life. You also have acknowledged the fact that you may be empty yourself, but are determined to change. Whatever it takes, you are determined to break the cycle and be a full well for your family and others who depend on you. Becoming a full well means taking back control of your life, and that may mean dealing first with control issues.

Give Me the Remote

Many people with empty well syndrome also have control issues in their lives. It could be anyone: a father, a mother, a son, a daughter, a grandparent, a spouse, a boss, a pastor, or a teacher. Since they cannot control the circumstances of their relationship with their empty well, they try to compensate by seeking control—often excessive control—in other areas.

Whether at home, in the workplace, or elsewhere, they may become authoritarian, domineering, "my way or the highway" type of people, micromanaging everything in an effort to control every aspect of their lives and the lives of those within their sphere of influence, whether spouse, children, employees, congregation, or whoever.

The empty well syndrome often comes with control issues.

Often they are workaholics and obsessed with success and perfection, and they demand the same from their subordinates. Consequently, they have little tolerance for failure or for work standards that fall short of their own extreme ideal. Where subordinates are concerned, they often mistake fear for respect, since both of these present themselves the same way. Therefore, they envision themselves as effective leaders because their subordinates follow and obey without question. Their word is law and they are often blind to how such an authoritarian approach tends to squelch creativity and shut down valuable input and interaction.

At the root of most control issues lies the fundamental issue of *insecurity*. Few of us truly understand the depth of the influence that our relationship with our primary "well" has on our lives. How well we relate to our main emotional caregiver will significantly affect how well we relate to other people, not to mention how we view the world around us. Many empty well people, regardless of the bold, confident, "I've got it all together" demeanor they may display, suffer from a basic core of fear and insecurity based on the fundamental failure of their relationship with their empty well. Their insecurity in this relationship feeds a general insecurity about all relationships and situations in life. After all, if this most fundamental of relationships failed for them, what's to keep all the others from failing as well?

An authoritarian, domineering personality frequently masks an inner core of fear and insecurity. Such individuals *must* maintain control. Otherwise, in their minds, everything will fly apart just like that basic relationship with their empty well. Maintaining control is also a way of reassuring themselves of their power.

What about you? Is control an issue in your life? Are you a "control freak," always having to be in charge in every situation? Are you a manipulator or a schemer? Even when you are not in charge, do you look for ways to maneuver or manipulate circumstances or people in order to take over, even if it's just in the background? Are people you associate with regularly, such as family members, co-workers, or subordinates, afraid to cross you or disagree with you? Do you feel personally threatened when your ideas are challenged or when another strong personality is present?

How would the people who know you best describe your personality? Would they say you were easygoing? Tolerant? Sensitive to other people's feelings and needs? Receptive to other ideas and opinions even when they run contrary to your own? Open to change? Or would they portray you as author-itarian? Harsh? Domineering? Intolerant? Insensitive and unfeeling? Oblivious to the feelings and needs of others? Hostile to ideas and opinions other than your own? Resistant to change?

Taking control of your life is not the same thing as being a control freak. If you are a controlling person, your obsession with control may real-ly be a *reaction* to a negative experi-ence in your life—perhaps more than one—an experience over which you had no control and which left you feeling helpless, powerless, and deeply hurt. Even now that experi-ence, however long ago, continues to control you because it determines how you think and act today. Virtually everything you do is designed to protect yourself against ever being hurt or help-less like that again.

Before you can "take control," you have to stop "controlling."

By contrast, taking control of your life means letting go of your controlling "instinct." Instead of reacting to the negative experiences of your past and thereby allowing them to control you still, when you take control, you make a deliberate deci-sion to break with that past: "Yes, that happened and it hurt, but I am moving on with my life now. I am not going to allow those things to control me anymore." Before you can "take control," you have to stop "controlling."

Essentially, it is the difference between *reaction* and *response*. Controllers react according to protective and defen-sive apparatus put in place long ago. People who take control of their lives learn to give an appropriate response according to the need or demand of the situation. They are truly free because, even if they cannot always control what happens in life, they can control how they respond. Their behavior today is not bound or determined by what happened to them yesterday or last year or when they were children. Once codependent, they have moved ahead to self-determination.

Positive or Negative Control?

Perhaps the greatest risk in taking control of your life again is that you can move in either a negative or positive direction. Depending on the level of your pain or resentment or on how well you have dealt with the negative emotional elements related to your empty well experience, you may choose thought and behavior patterns that are either constructive or self-destructive, that will either help you or harm you.

The empty well syndrome often reveals a root of rejection.

It is like being at home alone and picking up the remote to watch some television. No one is there to see you or to either direct or control your choices. You are on your own, free to watch whatever you choose. You can choose to watch the sleazy stuff like the sex channels and the "trash" talk shows that will poison your mind, or you can choose a good movie or documentary or other positive programming that will edify your mind. The choice is yours. Are you ready to handle the remote?

Give Me the Remote

Deep inside every person suffering from the empty well syndrome is a common root of rejection. Somewhere along the way in one way or another they have been rejected by the person or persons who matter the most. Rejection causes pain, and repeated rejection only intensifies it. Over time, that pain can mutate into resentment, bitterness, or even hatred toward those who rejected them. Because empty well syndrome people generally feel powerless in relating to the empty wells in their lives, their negative thoughts and feelings are directed elsewhere. They come out in many different ways, quite often in various forms of self-destructive behavior.

When we are rejected by the empty well in our lives, the need that drove us to them in the first place is still there, and we will start looking around for someone or something else to satisfy that need and to fill that void in our hearts. Like the man in the desert at the beginning of Chapter Four, sometimes we can get so thirsty that we are willing even to drink contaminated water just to quench our thirst.

It is our nature as humans, when hurt or rejected, to turn to destructive rather than constructive behavior. We may start drinking or doing drugs or engaging in free sex, or we could become risk-takers or thrill-seekers—anything to fill the void. Sometimes it takes the form of open defiance as we deliberately rebel against and disobey our parents (or whoever our empty well happens to be) in an effort to declare or prove our independence from them. Even in this defiance, however, our lives are still shaped by our empty wells because we do what we do precisely because they don't want us to.

Do you see the trap? Negative behavior never liberates; it only drags you down deeper. Rather than setting you free, to choose self-destructive behavior is to choose to remain in bondage, condemned to repeat the cycle of rejection, hurt, and bitterness. It strips you of any power to change that you may once have had.

> *Reject the destructive in favor of the constructive.*

Overcoming the empty well syndrome means rejecting destructive choices and behavior in favor of constructive choices and behavior. Taking control of your life is a very mature decision to choose the good over the bad and the positive over the negative. It is a deliberate choice to go against your nature and the patterns of your past. At heart, taking control of your life is to choose freedom over bondage; it is a determination to find full, healthy wells to quench your thirst and replace the empty wells that no longer sustain you.

This is not always an easy process. It takes time and a lot of hard and diligent work. Making the adjustment to a new way of thinking and acting is often painful in itself, but there is no other way to freedom. Laurie, a young woman who is going through this process now, testifies to its difficulty, but persists because she believes the end result will be worth the effort. Here is what she told me:

> I spent eight years in a relationship with someone who simply did not know how to give. It was eight years of my sacrificing, giving up, and giving in with very little in return. One day I realized that I was dying emotionally and had to move on. Before long, I found myself in another relationship that was very similar to the first. The fortunate difference this time is that my

husband recognizes the need to change. Still, I find myself asking the question, "What is it about me that led me to this place? What is it about my spouse that led him to the place where he is?"

After much consideration, I came to the conclusion that it is a father's responsibility to meet the physical, emotional, and spiritual needs of his children. If he does not, then the children may get stuck at that place in their lives. Even as they grow to adulthood physically, they may remain children emotionally, making them incapable of filling the emotional needs of their own families as well as others around them.

When we grow up "emotionally disabled," we cannot form healthy relationships. We take but we do not know how to give. We are constantly looking for someone to fill us, but because we are empty we do not have anything to give back. Since our fathers did not fill us when we were thirsty, we search for someone else to quench our thirst as adults. Although we realize that we are in a self-destructive pattern, unless we know the cause we may not be able to reach the solution.

I am happy to say that my family is working toward healing and restoration, but it has proven to be a very painful process for us all. Among other things, it has required that I recognize that no man on earth can fill the void that my father neglected. My husband has had to recognize the same thing in his life. Ultimately, the road to our recovery has required us to release one another of our fathers' debts.

After many years in failed or ailing relationships and not understanding why, Laurie has decided to take control of her life. The emotional health and welfare of her marriage and her family are too important to risk by allowing the negative cycle of her life to continue. Although she recognized her father's failures as the central cause of her problems, she also acknowledges her own responsibility on the road to recovery. She understands that she cannot hold him responsible for her own unhappiness, low self-esteem, or low sense of self-worth. Those things may have started with her father's neglect, but whether or not they continue to dominate her life is up to her. She has chosen to change, no matter how much pain is involved in the process. She has taken charge of the remote, committed to determine her own destiny rather than allow someone else to set it for her. After a lifetime of guilt, regret, and uncertainty, Laurie is learning to love herself again.

Low self-esteem commonly accompanies the empty well syndrome.

Learn to Love Yourself

Developing a healthy self-image is one of the most positive action steps you can make in taking control of your life. Low self-esteem is a very common problem with empty well syndrome people because their sense of self-worth is so tightly bound emotionally to the love, affirmation, and approval of the primary "well" in their lives. The discovery that this well is empty usually devastates them. Sometimes it takes years to recover, and some never do.

Over the past 25 or 30 years, our society has produced an enormous amount of literature on self-image and self-esteem issues. Self-esteem has been one of the hottest topics of our generation. We have heard so much in recent years about "empowerment" and "enablement," about not being a victim anymore, and about breaking our co-dependency. In some quarters it appears that the primary focus of this generation is on building ourselves up any way we can.

The central flaw in so much of our emphasis on self-esteem is its narcissism: Self-love becomes self-worship. Character flaws and moral failures are either dismissed as irrelevant in a modern age or attributed to a bad environment or a disadvantaged childhood. Personal responsibility is minimized in favor of the freedom to live however we please with no guilt and no commitment and no inconvenient divine sanctions. After all, nothing is more important than our self and its indulgences.

That is not the kind of self-image I am talking about. Society's self-esteem is superficial and shallow, a razor-thin veneer of happiness and optimism covering over a corrupt and deeply hurting spirit that is propped up by self-indulgent human platitudes that tell us over and over, "You're okay, you're okay, you're okay," when deep inside we know we are not.

I am talking about a self-image based not on who we think we are but on who God thinks we are; not on how we see ourselves but on how God sees us; not on what we see in ourselves but on what God sees in us.

A healthy self-image begins with a clear and accurate understanding of who we really are. What is our nature as human beings? To answer that we must turn not to the politically correct and culturally acceptable maxims of our day that speak of the innate goodness of man, but to the unchanging truth of God's Word. Simply stated, the Bible says we are *sinners*. That is our essential nature. It means we stand in open rebellion against God and in every way miss the mark of what He intended for us when He created us. As sinners, we also stand under God's judgment. The Word of God leaves no doubt as to our condition:

> *We all, like sheep, have gone astray, each of us has turned to his own way* (Isaiah 53:6a).

> *All have turned aside, they have together become corrupt; there is no one who does good, not even one* (Psalm 14:3).

> *Everyone has turned away, they have together become corrupt; there is no one who does good, not even one* (Psalm 53:3).

> *For all have sinned and fall short of the glory of God* (Romans 3:23).

It was not always this way. In the beginning, mankind enjoyed perfect fellowship with God. Adam and Eve walked in an unbroken love relationship with God and completely fulfilled all that He had designed them for—until the day they disobeyed Him. Since that day, all of humanity has been subject to a severed relationship with God, our Father. Because we were designed and created to love God, we all have a God-shaped hole in our hearts that can be filled only by Him. God is love, and without that relationship with Him, we seek continually to fill that void whatever way we can, not always understanding that God deliberately placed that void in us so that we would seek Him. God, in His divine wisdom, put a "Father-hunger" in each of us that we seek to fill every day of our lives. His desire is for us to discover that He alone can give us what we seek.

God alone can give us what we seek.

Another truth that the Bible makes perfectly clear is that, even though we are sinners, God loves us and wants to restore our severed relationship. That is why He sent Jesus, His only Son. Although He was without sin, Jesus took our sins upon Himself and died in our place so that we could be forgiven and have eternal life. Jesus died so that we could live:

> *For God so loved the world that he gave his one and only Son, that whoever believes in him shall not perish but have eternal life* (John 3:16).

> *But God demonstrates his own love for us in this: While we were still sinners, Christ died for us* (Romans 5:8).

Look at the complete verse of Isaiah 53:6:

> *We all, like sheep, have gone astray, each of us has turned to his own way; and the LORD has laid on him [Jesus] the iniquity of us all* (Isaiah 53:6).

We are sinners, yet God loves us enough that He sent His Son to die for us. Why? Why does God love us? First of all, it is God's nature to love because He *is* love. Second, God created us in His image and, even in our sin, a spark, a glimmer of that image remains and is precious to Him. God loves us not because of who we are in our own merits but because of who we are (or can become) in Him.

A healthy self-image is based first on the knowledge that we are sinners and second on the awareness that God loves us anyway and wants to restore our severed relationship with Him, which is something only He can do. We can learn to love ourselves not because of who we are on our own, but by rediscovering who we are in Christ: children of God, royal citizens of His kingdom, and forgiven sinners saved by the grace of God. Created in God's image and still bearing a spark of His divine nature, we are precious in His sight and worthy not because of what we have done but because of what Christ did for us and because of what God knows we can do and be in His power.

Jesus said that the first and greatest commandment is to love God with all our heart, soul, mind, and strength, and the second is to love our neighbor as ourselves. It is only when we come to understand who we are in Christ that we can trade our self-loathing for a healthy self-love based on His work of grace in us. Only then can we truly love God and our neighbor as we should. Only then do we have a *safe* power in which to pick up the remote and take control of our lives in a positive way.

If you are reading this book and have never yet taken the step of turning to Christ in faith, I urge you to do so now. Without Jesus you will never be able to fully take control of your life or fully satisfy the hunger and thirst in your heart because they can be satisfied only by Him. Turn from your sin—acknowledge that you are a sinner and confess that to God. Then, in a conscious decision and act of faith, acknowledge

Jesus Christ as your Savior, the One who saves you from your sins, and your Lord, the One to whom you surrender control of your life. Faith in Christ will restore your severed relationship with God, your Father. Without this restored relationship, full recovery, healing, and freedom are not possible.

Take Control By Letting Go

Earlier I said that in order to take control of your life you have to give up your controlling instinct, your obsession or need to control everything, because it is a sign of your bondage to the negative experiences of your past. True freedom in life comes in the ability to make decisions based on where you want to go rather than on where you have been.

True freedom comes when you can make decisions based on where you want to go.

In a similar way, taking control of your life really means letting go and giving control to the Lord. By yourself you lack the capability to direct your life the way you should. The same is true for all of us. Christ alone has the wisdom and the power to make your life what it ought to be. He alone can bring you the peace and fulfillment you have been longing for. Only in Him does life truly make sense.

Proverbs 3:5-6 says, *"Trust in the LORD with all your heart and lean not on your own understanding; in all your ways acknowledge him, and he will make your paths straight."* In other words, don't trust in your own wisdom. Trust the Lord completely, and He will lead you in the way you should go. He is the source of all wisdom. The New Testament writer James said, *"If any of you lacks wisdom, he should ask God, who gives generously to all without finding fault, and it will be given to him"* (James 1:5).

It would be foolish to give control of your life to someone who could not lead you wisely or who would not care about what happens to you. You don't have to worry about that when you give your life to Jesus. The Bible pictures Jesus as a Good Shepherd who faithfully leads His flock:

> *"The man who enters by the gate is the shepherd of his sheep. The watchman opens the gate for him, and the sheep listen to his voice. He calls his own sheep by name and leads them out. When he has brought out all his own, he goes on ahead of them, and his sheep follow him because they know his voice."...Therefore Jesus said again, "I tell you the truth, I am the gate for the sheep....I am the gate; whoever enters through me will be saved. He will come in and go out, and find pasture. The thief comes only to steal and kill and destroy; I have come that they may have life, and have it to the full. I am the good shepherd. The good shepherd lays down his life for the sheep....I am the good shepherd; I know my sheep and my sheep know me—just as the Father knows me and I know the Father—and I lay down my life for the sheep"* (John 10:2-4, 7, 9-11, 14-15).

As the Good Shepherd, Jesus fulfills what King David the psalmist wrote:

> *The LORD is my shepherd, I shall not be in want. He makes me lie down in green pastures, he leads me beside quiet waters, he restores my soul. He guides me*

in paths of righteousness for his name's sake. Even though I walk through the valley of the shadow of death, I will fear no evil, for you are with me; your rod and your staff, they comfort me (Psalm 23:1-4).

Take control of your life by giving control of it to Christ. He will never lead you astray. His guidance will lead you to green pastures, quiet waters, the paths of righteousness, and restoration of your soul. Pick up the remote for your life and give it to Jesus. With Him in control, you will never have to worry about how your life will unfold.

Become the Change You Want to See

Reform always begins at home. It's easy to point a finger at someone else's faults, but when we do we often forget that there are three fingers pointing back at us. It's just as easy to blame our problems and flaws on our environment or our disadvantaged circumstances or our upbringing or our abusive father or inattentive mother or any number of other scapegoats—anywhere but on ourselves. We will never be able

Reform always begins at home.

to move forward as long as we blame somebody else for our lack of progress. Only when we reach the place of being willing to accept responsibility for our own attitudes and actions will we be ready for true change.

Jesus said:

Why do you look at the speck of sawdust in your brother's eye and pay no attention to the plank in your

*own eye? How can you say to your brother, "Let me
take the speck out of your eye," when all the time there
is a plank in your own eye? You hypocrite, first take
the plank out of your own eye, and then you will see
clearly to remove the speck from your brother's eye*
(Matthew 7:3-5).

Change will not come automatically. Neither will it occur by
accident. Change is a choice. Remember Laurie's story? Laurie
came to realize that her situation would never change until she
decided to change it and committed herself to doing everything
necessary to make it happen. Many folks never change their
unhappy and self-defeating circumstances because they think
change is too difficult. It is much easier simply to stay where
they are. Sometimes it is because they are lazy and lack motivation. Other times it is because discouragement over repeated
rejection and failure has stripped them of hope.

Mahatma Gandhi, advocate of non-violent resistance and
champion of India's independence from the British Empire,
said, "*Become the change you want to see in the world.*" In
other words, if you want to change the world, start by changing yourself. Take the initiative. Don't wait for others. Be a
pacesetter rather than a trend-follower. A biblical parallel to
Gandhi's words would be Jesus' statement commonly known
as the "Golden Rule": "*So in everything, do to others what
you would have them do to you, for this sums up the Law
and the Prophets*" (Matthew 7:12). Treat others the way you
want to be treated, even if they have not treated you that way.
Don't sit in a snit and say, "Well, he treated me bad, so I'm
going to do the same to him." Set the example. Become the
change you want to see in others.

Give Me the Remote

If you are struggling with empty well syndrome, here are some tips to help you on the road to change. First, *stop living your life through someone else's eyes or for someone else's dreams and expectations.* Your life is yours. God gave it to you for a purpose and only you can fulfill God's purpose for your life. As long as you continue to seek affirmation, approval, and recognition from an empty well, all you will do is spin your wheels and your life will be on hold. Accept the fact that you may never get what you need and want from that well, and resolve to move on with your life. Don't waste your life, your resources, and God's plan for you by running continually after something you may never get.

Second, *stop trying to change your empty well into a full well.* No matter who your empty well is—your father, your mother, your grandfather, your grandmother, whoever—you will be beating your head against a brick wall trying to get him or her to change. It won't work. The only water you will ever get out of an empty well is the water you put in it. Depending on your empty well, even that water may come back to you contaminated. Be careful how you use the precious water you are carrying in your own well. Many people are depending on you to be a well for them. What will they do if you use up all your water trying to change the person who should have been a full well for you but wasn't?

Third, *become the change you want to see.* No matter what situation you are in and no matter how empty you may feel right now, you have the power to change. If you are a believer, a follower of Jesus Christ, then His Holy Spirit resides in you and has endowed you with the power to change the direction of your life. You don't have to stay the way you are. You don't have to remain empty. You can break the cycle and loose the grip that your empty well person has had on you all these years. You start to become the change the moment you decide that even though your well was never full for you, you are determined to do everything you can to be a full well for your family and anybody else who looks to you and depends on you.

So pick up that remote. Take control of your life by letting go of your controlling instincts and by releasing control into the Lord's hands. You *can* become the change you want to see, but only when you make the deliberate, conscious choice to do so regardless of the cost. And one of the costliest things you may have to do in this process is to forgive your empty well person—to let him or her off the hook. Is that a price you are willing to pay?

Chapter Six

LET IT GO

orrie ten Boom spent the first 50 years of her life living quietly in Haarlem, Holland, the city of her birth. Along with her older sister, Betsie, Corrie lived with her father and an aunt who had moved in to help out after their mother died. Their old house, two adjoining buildings that had been converted into one residence, was also physically connected to the shop where Corrie's father had his watchmaking business. Corrie learned the art of watchmaking by helping her father in the shop and eventually became the first licensed woman watchmaker in Holland.

More important to the ten Booms than watchmaking, however, was their steadfast faith in Christ. He was the center of their lives and of everything they did. Corrie's father loved to read and discuss the Bible with his customers, many of whom were Jewish. Bible reading and prayer were daily activities for the ten Boom family.

In 1940, the firestorm of World War II engulfed Holland as it did the rest of western Europe. Under the heel of Nazi tyranny, daily life for the Dutch people descended into a nightmare of fear, uncertainty, and middle-of-the-night raids and arrests. It was especially hard on the Jews of Holland, who were subject at any time to arrest and deportation to concentration camps.

Because of opportunity and their strong Christian beliefs and values, Corrie and her family became involved in the Dutch resistance movement, opening their home as a "hiding place" for Jews fleeing the Nazis. Before being exposed and arrested, the ten Booms were instrumental in assisting scores of Jews to escape the country. After their arrest Corrie, Betsie, their father, and other members of the family were sent to concentration camps.

Corrie and Betsie ended up in Ravensbruck where, amid the horror, brutality, and spiritual darkness of the camp, they brought the bright light of Christ and the love of God. As Corrie relates in her best-selling book, *The Hiding Place*, miracles large and small abounded in the camp as many prisoners discovered God's love and the light of eternal life in Christ in the midst of a place that was truly a hell on earth.

Betsie died at Ravensbruck; Corrie's father and a nephew died in other camps. Inexplicably, Corrie herself was released. She later learned that her release was due to a "clerical error," and that a week later an order came down for all the women in the camp her age and older to be put to death. After the war and for the rest of her life, Corrie traveled the world as a self-described "tramp for the Lord," sharing her story and her experiences but most of all, sharing the message of God's love and forgiveness and of salvation through faith in Christ.

Even for such a saintly person as Corrie ten Boom, dealing with the pain of the past was not always easy. Even as she spoke to others about love and forgiveness, she sometimes struggled with her own bitterness. In her book, *Tramp for the Lord,* she relates one such instance:

> *Even Corrie ten Boom dealt with the issue of forgiveness.*

> It was in a church in Munich that I saw him—a balding, heavy-set man in a gray overcoat, a brown felt hat clutched between his hands. People were filing out of the basement room where I had just spoken, moving along the rows of wooden chair to the door at the rear. It was 1947 and I had come from Holland to defeated Germany with the message that God forgives.
>
> ...I saw him, working his way forward against the others. One moment I saw the overcoat and the brown hat; the next, a blue uniform and a visored cap with its skull and crossbones. It came back with a rush: the huge room with its harsh overhead lights; the pathetic pile of dresses and shoes in the center of the floor; the shame of walking naked past this man....The place was Ravensbruck and the man making his way forward had been a guard—one of the most cruel guards.
>
> Now he was in front of me, hand thrust out: "A fine message, Fraulein! How good it is to know that, as you say, all our sins are at the bottom of the sea!"

And I, who had spoken so glibly of forgiveness, fumbled in my pocketbook rather than take that hand. He would not remember me, of course...

But I remembered him and the leather crop swinging from his belt. I was face-to-face with one of my captors and my blood seemed to freeze.

"You mentioned Ravensbruck in your talk," he was saying. "I was a guard there...."

"But since that time," he went on, "I have become a Christian. I know that God has forgiven me for the cruel things I did there, but I would like to hear it from your lips as well. Fraulein,"—again the hand came out—"will you forgive me?"

And I stood there—I whose sins had again and again to be forgiven—and could not forgive. Betsie had died in that place—could he erase her slow terrible death simply for the asking?

It could not have been many seconds that he stood there—hand held out—but to me it seemed hours as I wrestled with the most difficult thing I had ever had to do.

For I had to do it—I knew that. The message that God forgives has a prior condition: that we forgive those who have injured us....

I knew it not only as a commandment of God, but as a daily experience....

And still I stood there with the coldness clutching my heart. But forgiveness is not an emotion—I knew that too. Forgiveness is an act of the will, and the will can function regardless of the temperature of the heart.

"Jesus, help me!" I prayed silently. "I can lift my hand. I can do that much. You supply the feeling."

And so woodenly, mechanically, I thrust my hand into the one stretched out to me. And as I did, an incredible thing took place. The current started in my shoulder, raced down my arm, sprang into our joined hands. And then this healing warmth seemed to flood my whole being, bringing tears to my eyes.

"I forgive you, brother!" I cried. "With all my heart."

For a long moment we grasped each other's hands, the former guard and the former prisoner. I had never known God's love so intensely as I did then. But even so, I realized it was not my love. I had tried, and did not have the power. It was the power of the Holy Spirit as recorded in Romans 5:5, "...because the love of God is shed abroad in our hearts by the Holy Ghost which is given unto us."[1]

What Do You Mean, "Forgive"?

Corrie ten Boom understood what many Christians today, I am afraid, do not: Forgiveness is a fundamental spiritual principle that affects everything from our physical health to the quality of our relationship with Christ. She knew that she had no right to continue talking to others about God's love and forgiveness unless she was willing and able to extend forgiveness to someone who had hurt her. At the same time she knew that no false, shallow gesture or the superficial words "I forgive you" would do. Forgiving this former concentration camp guard who had caused so much pain and who had hurt

Corrie and so many other people took a power beyond her own, a thorough work of God in her from the inside out, supplying her with that which she could not supply herself—the ability to love and forgive her former enemy and welcome him not just as a friend but as a brother in Christ. That is a spiritual transformation that cannot be explained in terms of human psychology.

Forgiveness is a matter of life and death.

Many people today act as though forgiveness is no big deal. That is because they do not understand what true forgiveness really is or what it involves. Forgiveness is not only a matter of health but also a matter of life and death. Psychiatric wards and mental hospitals all over our country are filled with people who have unresolved forgiveness issues. Some of them are people who need to forgive but won't do it, while others need to be forgiven but can't find it. Forgiveness issues of one kind or another are the primary factors behind many, perhaps even most cases of mental or emotional illness.

Unforgiveness destroys friendships, severs relationships, tears apart families and churches, eats away at our spirits like a cancer, sows discord and suspicion among brothers, and breeds hatred and resentment that can last a lifetime or, in the case of clashing ethnic or racial groups, even centuries.

Nothing affects our spiritual life more negatively than an unresolved forgiveness matter. More than any other single factor, unforgiveness lies at the heart of most spiritual problems and the failure of so many believers to grow in Christ and experience the fullness of life in Him that He wants them to have. Our spiritual health rises or falls depending on how we handle the matter of forgiveness. Is it any surprise, then, that God's Word would have so much to say on the subject?

When Jesus taught His followers to pray, He gave them a model prayer, known as the Lord's Prayer, which included this petition:

> *Forgive us our debts, as we also have forgiven our debtors* (Matthew 6:12).

A couple of verses later, He elaborated on the importance of forgiveness:

> *For if you forgive men when they sin against you, your heavenly Father will also forgive you. But if you do not forgive men their sins, your Father will not forgive your sins* (Matthew 6:14-15).

Did you catch that? *Our* experience of forgiveness hinges on our willingness and obedience in forgiving others. If something seems not quite right in your relationship with God, try examining your heart to see if you have a forgiveness problem. It is impossible to be right with God when you are not right with another person, at least as far as it depends on you. Jesus said:

> *Therefore, if you are offering your gift at the altar and there remember that your brother has something against you, leave your gift there in front of the altar. First go and be reconciled to your brother; then come and offer your gift* (Matthew 5:23-24).

Reconciliation often involves forgiveness and is so important that the Lord has said we should postpone worship until we have achieved it (or have done everything in our power to do so). At the same time, it takes two people to reconcile. If you have a forgiveness issue with another person, and that person is not willing to reconcile, there is only so much you can do. Still, you will never know until you try. Jesus' point in these verses is that it is our responsibility to initiate reconciliation when we become aware of the problem, even if it is not our fault. However, the phrase *"your brother has something against you"* seems to imply that the "brother" in question is the offended one. The meaning is clear: If you have offended a brother and stand in need of his forgiveness, don't try to worship God until you have settled the matter. To do otherwise is to be guilty of hypocrisy.

If you are the offended one and someone has hurt you and needs to be forgiven, don't wait for that person to come to you. Take the initiative and extend forgiveness to that person, even if he or she has not asked for it. This is critical not only for his or her spiritual welfare but for yours as well. Jesus said:

> *And when you stand praying, if you hold anything against anyone, forgive him, so that your Father in heaven may forgive you your sins* (Mark 11:25).

Refusal to forgive betrays an absence of love both for our brother and for God:

> *If anyone says, "I love God," yet hates his brother, he is a liar. For anyone who does not love his brother, whom he has seen, cannot love God, whom he has not seen* (1 John 4:20).

A forgiving spirit is foundational to everything else. No true worship, spiritual growth, healing, freedom, or recovery is possible without it.

"But, Mark," you may protest, "I can't forgive this person! He (or she) has hurt me too badly."

That's not completely true. Like Corrie ten Boom, you may indeed lack the power within yourself to forgive, but that does not relieve you of the responsibility to do so. Forgiveness is a command, not an option; it is an act of the will, not an emotion. If the desire of your heart is to live and walk in obedience to Christ, you *must* forgive, and He can give you the power to do so. To say, "I can't forgive," is dishonest; what you are really saying is, "I won't forgive." Take the first step. With an act of the will, resolve to forgive, and trust the Lord for the power.

If you want to live and walk with Christ, you must forgive.

First, Forgive Yourself

Before you can forgive the empty well person in your life (or anybody else) you may need to deal with the matter of learning to forgive yourself. Now that you have come to the point of self-discovery and have acknowledged the fact of the empty well syndrome in your life, you may have personal anger issues to resolve. Maybe you're thinking, *How could I waste so much time and so many years going back again and again to that empty well, always hoping to find something good there, even though I knew I wouldn't? Why have I let that person control my life and my emotions for so long? Why have I let myself become co-dependent? I can hardly think for myself or act on my own. How did this happen? I've wasted so many years and expended so many resources, and for what? After all this time, I finally realize that I have never been free, and now it may be too late.*

These kinds of feelings are common for someone who is beginning to move from co-dependency to self-determination. Regret over wasted years is often an immediate by-product of having our eyes opened and finally "seeing the light." The danger lies not in having these feelings and regrets, but in getting *stuck* there, spinning our wheels in a cycle of self-condemnation. Stop beating yourself up. Stop banging your head against the wall. All you will have to show for that are bruises and a headache. At the same time, don't deny that it happened, don't water it down, and don't sweep it under the rug. That's not recovery. Recovery means accepting what has happened and *moving on.* It means being able to say, "Yeah, that was then, but this is now, and things are different." The very fact that you have these feelings is actually proof that you have turned a corner in your life.

In his letter to the Philippian church, the apostle Paul revealed how he had learned the importance of letting go of the past and moving on:

> *But whatever was to my profit I now consider loss for the sake of Christ. What is more, I consider everything a loss compared to the surpassing greatness of knowing Christ Jesus my Lord, for whose sake I have lost all things. I consider them rubbish, that I may gain Christ and be found in him, not having a righteousness of my own that comes from the law, but that which is through faith in Christ—the righteousness that comes from God and is by faith....Not that I have already obtained all this, or have already been made perfect, but I press on to take hold of*

that for which Christ Jesus took hold of me. Brothers, I do not consider myself yet to have taken hold of it. But one thing I do: Forgetting what is behind and straining toward what is ahead, I press on toward the goal to win the prize for which God has called me heavenward in Christ Jesus (Philippians 3:7-9, 12-14).

Paul came to realize that everything he had done before coming to Christ—his striving to obey the Jewish law and live righteously on his own merits—was vain and useless. Only in Christ did he find what he was looking for. Although he wasted many years before he found the truth, Paul did not let that stop him. He set it all aside and pressed forward. You should do the same. If you have given your heart to Christ, He has forgiven you of your sins. Psalm 103:12 says that God has removed your sins from you as far as the east is from the west. Your past no longer stands in your way. Don't get stuck in a self-defeating cycle of regret and recrimination. Leave the past in the past and move ahead to a future of freedom and healing. Forgive yourself. Then you will be ready to forgive your empty well.

> *Leave the past in the past and move forward to a future of freedom.*

Forgiveness Means Letting Someone Off the Hook

Forgiveness is not always an easy process. Depending on the magnitude of the offense, forgiving the offender may be the hardest thing you have ever done. In our sinful nature, our fundamental impulse when hurt is to strike back. We want to even the score, to inflict on the offender as much pain as he or she inflicted on us. True forgiveness comes in letting the offender off the hook for hurting us, and that cuts against the grain of our human nature. Letting your offender off the hook means just that—you don't hold his offense on your "hook" to use against him later. Instead, you take it off the hook and throw it back in the water.

Forgiving may be the hardest thing you have ever done.

On the road to true forgiveness, there are two dangerous pitfalls of false forgiveness to watch out for. The first is minimizing the offense. Don't make the offense out for less than it is. Someone comes to you and says, "I'm sorry I hurt you. Will you forgive me?" and you reply, "That's okay; don't worry about it." If it truly *is* okay, that's one thing. If you truly took no offense then there is no need for forgiveness. On the other hand, if you truly were hurt, don't minimize the offense. Don't pretend that it's okay when it's not okay. That's not forgiveness. Minimizing the offense is not forgiveness because it lets *you* off the hook rather than the offender. Saying "Don't worry about it" is easier on you than accepting the responsibility to genuinely forgive the offender. When you honestly and truly forgive, you release your offender completely from the offense against you and hold nothing back to use against him or her later on: "Ah, but you remember when you did this to me...!" Don't minimize the offense. Let your offender off the hook.

Let It Go

The second pitfall is sweeping the offense under the rug, pretending that it never happened at all. This is worse than minimizing the offense. Now you have been hurt but you tell yourself you haven't been or you try to explain away the offender's actions by giving him or her the benefit of the doubt: "Surely he didn't mean to say that"; "Certainly she wasn't trying to hurt my feelings." It may well be that the offense was unintentional, but unintentional or not, your hurt is real. Don't pretend that it isn't there. Don't sweep it under the rug.

Repressed hurt grows in intensity and mutates into anger, resentment, bitterness, and rage. Your wound is so deep that all you can do is dwell on revenge. It never heals because you never let it. You keep pulling off the scab and digging at it. After a while, your pain becomes so familiar that it is like an old friend that you can't bear to part from. Your hurt is now a part of you and you can't imagine daily life without it. It feels like a cut that won't heal or a bruise that won't go away. It is like a bone spur in your foot that makes you limp because the irritation won't let you put all your weight on that foot. Eventually, if left unresolved, your hurt will push its way to the surface and you will end up taking it out not on the offender, but on innocent people around you, perhaps your spouse or your children. Don't sweep your pain under the rug. Don't pretend that it never happened.

There is tremendous power in letting your offender off the hook and in completely releasing him or her from the offense. Unforgiveness traps you in the past, binds your heart and mind to the offense, and ties you emotionally to the person who hurt you. True forgiveness liberates you as well as your offender. It frees you from your hurt and pain and from the sense of being tied to an emotional well that will never satisfy. As far as you are concerned, forgiveness frees your offender—your empty well person—to be him or herself, empty well and all, with no strings attached, no expectations in those areas, and no grudges or hard feelings on your part.

When you truly let it go, you will feel as though the greatest weight in the world has been lifted from your shoulders. By refusing to minimize the offense or sweep it under the rug and by truly letting it go, you empower yourself to move ahead to healing and wholeness.

Forgiveness Means Making Yourself Vulnerable Again

As with any worthwhile forward progress, learning to forgive carries an element of risk. Letting someone off the hook, choosing to forgive and to release an offense is risky because it means making yourself vulnerable again. That is why it is so important to learn to forgive yourself and to be at peace with yourself, for when you are at peace with yourself and your life, being vulnerable is not so scary a thing. Having a healthy self-image like we talked about in Chapter Five also helps take away the fear of vulnerability. Knowing who you are in Christ and immersing yourself in that reality banishes fear as you come to understand that there is no longer anyone or anything that can truly hurt you. Your life is wrapped up in Christ, not in your empty well person or anybody else. You can afford to let yourself be vulnerable because in Christ you are safe and secure and the way is open to you for healing and wholeness.

Part of the reason so many people cannot (or will not) forgive their empty well person or any other offender is because they have been hurt so many times that they are afraid and unwilling to let their guards down and make themselves vulnerable again. They think that if they do, they will only get hurt again. It is much easier to shut down emotionally, to cut themselves off from any close emotional involvement with others. By nursing their hurts and holding on to their grudges, they think they can exercise some control over the person or persons who hurt them. Someday, they dream, the opportunity will come to even the score.

True love is impossible without forgiveness.

Without forgiveness, true love is impossible because true love requires vulnerability. You cannot truly love anything or anyone without making yourself vulnerable; that's just how love is. The apostle Paul wrote of love:

> *Love is patient, love is kind. It does not envy, it does not boast, it is not proud. It is not rude, it is not self-seeking, it is not easily angered, it keeps no record of wrongs. Love does not delight in evil but rejoices with the truth. It always protects, always trusts, always hopes, always perseveres. Love never fails* (1 Corinthians 13:4-8a).

That's vulnerability. All the things we like to hold on to as protection against hurt—envy, boasting, pride, arrogance, self-seeking, grudge-holding—love lets go of. Love bares its heart to the world and says, "Come on, take your best shot; I will *still* love you!" Jesus did exactly that when He went to the cross. By crucifying the Son of God, who is love, sinful humanity took its best shot—and Jesus said, *"Father, forgive them, for they do not know what they are doing"* (Luke 23:34).

It is impossible to experience the full essence of true love, either giving or receiving, when we have safety nets strung up all around our hearts. Unless we are willing to take the risk of making ourselves vulnerable to the possibility of hurt, we will never know what true love is like. Love is risky because love can lead to hurt. None of us like to be hurt, so to protect our hearts from further pain, we quit loving, we quit forgiving, we quit changing, we quit doing anything that will put our hearts at risk again. The irony is that the very things we do to protect our hearts actually cause further damage because they make us unresponsive to love, and a heart without love is a sick heart.

As you forgive, and as you begin to make yourself more vulnerable, what you are actually doing is expanding your own heart to receive more. Once you start moving in the power of love and in the deeper level of understanding who you are in relationship with the Lord, and as you begin to let your offenders off the hook and completely release them, you set off a spiritual wind that begins to spin and move almost like a tornado, becoming so powerful that it can't help but affect the things and people around you. That's the power of love, forgiveness, and vulnerability.

Scars Are Evidence of Healing

Some people say that part of forgiving is forgetting. I disagree. Many wounds, whether physical or emotional, leave scars that last a lifetime. All we have to do is look at one of those scars and we can remember the wound that caused it. The difference comes in whether or not we remember the pain. We can look on our scars either as reminders of our pain or as evidence of our healing.

Let It Go

As a boy, I rode my bike everywhere. It seems like I never went anywhere without it. When I started my own lawn mowing business at the age of 13, I pulled the lawn mower behind my bike. We even built motor cross racetracks on the empty lot next to our house. I loved my bike and was a good rider.

One day when I was 14, however, I misjudged my environment. As I was riding my bike down the road, I heard a car coming up from behind. Thinking it was farther back than it was, I swerved to the left side of the street without looking back first. The car hit me. The next thing I knew, I was flying through the air and landed hard, skidding across the ground. All I was wearing was a pair of shorts, so the right side of my body was scraped from head to toe.

As I lay there immediately afterward, the first thought in my mind was, *How's my bike?* then, *How much trouble am I going to get into?* I was worried about what my dad might say about my bike and how much it would cost me to get it fixed. Forget my body. I knew it would heal, but I also knew I would probably have some scars.

The shock wore off quickly, and that's when the pain really began. I had never hurt so badly in my life! My body began to shake as I made my way home to get cleaned up and to remove the rocks that were ground into my skin. Talk about excruciating pain!

Over time, the scrapes scabbed over and began to heal. When the right side of your body is one huge scab, the slightest touch can make you climb the wall. But the scabs were a sign that I was healing. Eventually, the scabs fell off. Healing was complete. The pain was gone, but the scars remained.

Forgiveness makes it possible for us to look at the scars in our lives, and, instead of feeling the pain all over again, know that we are healed. Scars are evidence that healing has taken place. That is why when we forgive we don't forget. The scars will always be there to remind us of the wounds, but if healing has occurred, we won't feel any pain.

When you look at one of your scars, you can say, "You know what, this severed relationship, this pain that I endured from my empty well (or whoever) really hurt bad, but now I'm healed." If you don't remember what you were healed *from*, how can you have a testimony about it? Sometimes we want to cover up our scars—hide our past—but scars are there to remind us of where we have been, what we have come through, and the freedom that we enjoy today. Scars are evidence of healing—and survival.

Scars are evidence that healing has taken place.

What are the scars of your past? Abuse? Neglect? Abandonment? Invisibility? Don't try to hide them. Don't sweep them under the rug. Don't pretend there were never any issues in your life. There *were* issues. The true evidence of healing and the manifestation of God's forgiveness is when you can look at your scars and remember the events that occurred that gave them to you, but the pain is gone.

When we forgive, when we let it go, when we let somebody off the hook, something spiritual takes place in our lives. God does something supernatural in our hearts. I can't explain it, but when, in the Spirit of God, we offer up forgiveness and let someone go who has hurt us, a healing takes place. The sign of the healing is that the offense does not hurt us anymore. If you have to continually minimize the pain you went through in your life or pretend that it never happened, that's not healing; that's sweeping it under the rug and acting as if there never was an issue to start with.

Healing is a true manifestation. If your body has been sick and you are healed, you no longer worry about the sickness but focus on the fact that you are now well again. If you are wrestling with emotional pain in your life; if it is keeping you up at night so that you can't sleep, you have not been healed. You may be pretending to be healed, but it is only a sham. You've got to let it go—*truly* let it go.

When you let somebody off the hook in genuine forgiveness, giving up all control and all claim to resentment or offense, you free and empower that person to live life as he or she sees fit free of your expectations. At the same time, you bring God's empowerment into your own life—the empowerment to receive healing, restoration, and wholeness. It is a spiritual principle. That is the power of forgiveness and letting it go.

Endnote

1. Corrie ten Boom and Jamie Buckingham, *Tramp for the Lord*, 1974, Inspirational Press edition, *Corrie ten Boom: Her Story* (New York: Inspirational Press, a division of BBS Publishing Corporation. Published by arrangement with Chosen Books, Inc. and Fleming H. Revell, a division of Baker Book House Company, 1995), pp. 217-218.

Part Three:

OUT OF THE DESERT— THE JOURNEY TO HEALING AND FREEDOM

Chapter Seven

YOU HAVE A FATHER

W*alkabout*, a 1971 Australian film, tells the story of two schoolchildren, a teen-aged girl and her younger brother, who are stranded in the Australian outback after the death of their father. In the opening scenes of the film, the father picks his two children up from their exclusive private schools in a large city and takes them on a picnic several hours drive into the outback. No mother is present, creating the impression that the father is either divorced or widowed. After the picnic meal the young boy is sitting on a blanket playing and shooting an imaginary pistol. Suddenly, real gunshots are heard and puffs of dust rise from the ground near the boy. The children's crazed or depressed father has crouched behind their car and is firing a pistol at them.

Quickly, the girl manages to pull her brother to safety behind a large rock. Their father continues firing at them and calling out, "We must go now! We must go now!" Finally, when his children do not respond, he takes a gas can from the trunk of the car, douses the car with gasoline, and sets it on fire. Then, saying softly to himself, "I must go now," he lies down next to the burning vehicle and allows himself to be consumed by the flames.

With their father dead, the girl and her brother face a serious problem: survival. These "city folk" who have no clue how to live in the wild are now stranded in the remote outback, miles from anywhere, with very limited resources. After a couple of days struggling to find water, shelter, and food, the two children meet up with a young Aborigine male on his "walkabout," his rite of passage into manhood where he must survive on his own in the outback for a given period of time. Rescued from almost certain death, the girl and her brother throw in their lot with the young Aborigine and temporarily adopt his primitive ways. Because of his skills in living off the land, they are able to survive. By film's end, the two children have returned safely to the modern society from which they came but the Aborigine who befriended them, unable to cope with his clash with that society, dies.

The image I want you to see in this tale is that of two children stranded in the desert (outback) by a father who abandons them (dies). They are left to wander in the desert without a father, dependent only upon their own limited resources. A tragic situation? Absolutely! As a matter of fact, it is a double tragedy. First is the tragedy of children alone in a desert (either literally or figuratively) with no father (or mother) to guide them. They don't understand why they are there or why their father has left them there. The second tragedy is that of a father whose own emotional pain and mental torment are so bad that they drive him to do such a thing. His children become the innocent victims of his own problems and failures.

Like Father, Like Son

It always hurts when our father or mother or other principal caregiver does not give us what we need—love, affirmation, emotional support, or whatever—and we never understand why. "Doesn't Dad love me? Doesn't Mom care?" That hurt is very real and the neglect that causes it very wrong. However, because of the intensity of our own pain, we rarely stop to consider what pain or chaos or mental or emotional anguish they may be going through that could, if not justify, at least *explain* their action or inaction.

Almost every day now we read in the newspaper or hear on the news of a troubled parent somewhere doing violence to his or her children. In Oregon in 1983, Robert Galloway killed his wife and four children, then killed himself, apparently because his business was failing.

Susan Smith of Union, South Carolina, drowned her two young sons in 1994 by leaving them strapped in their car seats while she let the car roll into a lake and slowly sink. At the time of the murders Smith, a product of a very dysfunctional family, was going through a divorce and had recently been rejected by her boyfriend.

In 2001, Andrea Yates of Houston, Texas, methodically drowned her five young children in the bathtub. In addition to severe postpartum depression and a history of mental illness, Yates also had a strong preoccupation with the devil, telling investigators that she believed that killing her children was the only way to protect them from Satan.

Nothing could ever justify these horrific and tragic acts. My point is simply this: Most parents who harm their children, either actively through violence or passively through neglect, are deeply troubled themselves, often wrestling with parental abuse or neglect issues of their own. These tend to be self-perpetuating cycles, continuing from generation to generation until and unless they are stopped by deliberate action.

Whether good or bad, children tend to grow up to be like their parents.

Like the two children in *Walkabout*, children of *any age*, even adults, who are bereft of the emotional support of a parent, either through death or deprivation (as with an empty well) can be left feeling stranded in an emotional desert and ill-equipped to deal with the situation. They may be the children of empty wells or they may be empty wells themselves. Because of the cyclic nature of this problem, the two are interrelated. People who *are* empty wells usually are also the *children* of empty wells. Whether good or bad, children tend to grow up to be like their parents. In other words, like father, like son (or like mother, like daughter).

This cycle is demonstrated clearly in the experience of a young man named Steve, which he shared with a professional counselor during a session:

"Dad was a driver. He worked long and diligently, and he expected his children to do the same...If I didn't do something exactly the way he wanted it done—though I really tried to do a good job—he'd let me have it. I can remember only one time when I was growing up that he put an affirming hand on my shoulder. But he put his hand on my backside a few more times than that!"

"Did you ever spend much time with his father, your granddad?" I asked.

Steve responded instantly with a look of revelation. "You know, I did, and he was a crotchety old goat. He always seemed to have something to say about every-body, and it wasn't very complimentary! He even gave his grandchildren a pretty rough time."

Steve went on to say, "I don't like to admit it, but I treat my children the same way my father treated me and the same way his father treated him. I hate it! And I feel so guilty about it!"[1]

What works in Steve's favor is that he is aware of the prob-lem. He sees himself becoming an empty well just like his father and grandfather, and he wants to change. He wants to break the cycle so it won't continue with his own children. As long as he keeps that perspective, there is hope.

The "Father-Shaped Hole"

In the end, there is simply no substitute for parental love and support and affirmation. Who can deny, for example, the priceless value and nurturing warmth of a mother's love? Nothing can compare to it. Thousands of poems throughout the ages and thousands of years of human experience alike attest to the matchless virtues of the love of a mother.

The love of a father is just as important. Although some segments of our society in recent years have begun to devalue the role and importance of the father in a child's life, this flies in the face of overwhelming evidence to the contrary. At the same

Where are all the fathers?

time, however, the number of fatherless homes in our country is approaching epidemic proportions in some places. Today there are perhaps more single mothers than at any other time in our history. There are always exceptions, of course, but by and large, the single moms in our country do a bang-up job against great odds, working hard to raise their children well while trying to fill a second role—the father's role—that they were never meant to fill.

For the sake of balance and fairness, let me hasten to say also that there are many single fathers doing a wonderful job juggling between their careers and pulling double duty as both mom and dad to growing kids.

Generally speaking, however, father absenteeism is rising at an alarming rate. Where are all the fathers? I said earlier that out of the 700 young people in my youth ministry, 80 percent are fatherless. A study by the University of Maryland found that the most relevant factor behind violent crime and burglary in a community is not race or poverty but the percentage of households without fathers. National surveys of prison inmates reveal that 60 percent of rapists, 72 percent of adolescent murderers, and 70 percent of all inmates serving long prison terms grew up in homes where no father was present.

Could the statistics be any plainer? Fathers make a difference. *Everybody needs a father.* I said in Chapter One that we all have a love-shaped hole in our hearts. We also have a *father-shaped* hole in our hearts, a hole that only a father can fill. One of the reasons we have so many messed-up kids today is because their fathers are absent, either physically or emotionally, and these kids try to find other things to fill the gaping hole that absence has left in their hearts. The fathers are absent because *their* fathers were absent. Now the children are empty as well, and the cycle continues, cursing another generation to the barren desert of emotional dysfunction and despair.

A father's presence is so important that if we lack a father or a fatherly influence in our lives, we will look for a substitute, a surrogate father if you will. If necessary, we will turn to fantasy and make one up.

Chris Brewer, former NFL star who played for the Chicago Bears and the Denver Broncos, never knew his father. He shared with me this story from his childhood that shows the effect of an absent father in the life of a child but also points to a powerful solution:

> A three-year-old boy can't tell the difference between black and white TV and color TV nor does he care. A three-year-old boy has a hard time telling the difference between reality and make-believe.
>
> For two years, I had it perfect. My dad was the biggest man in town. He was strong yet without violence. He took care of every situation. He was kind and compassionate and seemed to love my brother and me without question, not because we did anything special, but just because he loved us. Even when my brother "Opie" got into trouble, he still loved us.
>
> Every day my brother and I would go fishing with "Pa," though I remember rarely ever eating fish. "Too

many bones," my mama would say. In spite of the fact that I couldn't whistle—I'm still not that good at it— when I heard the whistling I always felt safe. I always tried to whistle along, and could never figure out why that made my mama laugh. So, I would try to whistle all the time just to see her laugh. To this very day, whenever I whistle that certain tune I still smile.

One day, I don't remember when except that I was about five years old, I discovered that there *was* a difference between black and white and color TV— between reality and make-believe.

Up until then I had had it perfect. Andy Taylor was my father, Liz Brewer was my mother, and Opie Taylor was my brother. When I realized that only the "Liz Brewer" part was true, it left a giant hole in my heart that I didn't know existed. How could I have known? I was only five years old and the hole didn't pierce the skin or break bone or rip muscle. That giant hole penetrated right through to my soul. I was left empty. Everything that Opie had, I thought I had. Then, suddenly, Andy was just Opie's dad and I didn't have one.

My journey in life had just gotten much tougher and I asked my mama where my dad was. Where he was didn't matter as much as why he wasn't here to take me fishing while we whistled that happy tune together. I needed someone to build me a bridge quickly so that I could get over this trauma I was facing. No one did. Mama did the best she knew how, but she wasn't Andy; and neither was my real father.

So here I stand, forty-two years old, and trying all those years since I was five to fill that hole, that emptiness in my heart. I tried so many things to make everything perfect again. No matter what I tried, nothing worked. Nothing, that is, until I met my *other* father, my heavenly Father. My emptiness wasn't filled right away but more like a small dipper filling a glass. At least I knew that sooner or later I would be filled and that was better than nothing. What God did right away was repair my heart. It was like sealing a hole in a broken cup or vase so that I could be poured into.

God let me know that, like a diesel fuel truck running out of diesel, I am carrying what I need and should not deliver it to everyone else to the point of leaving myself empty. So many lessons to learn as I am still being filled!

I'm not alone. I see so many who are empty like I was, people who have everything the world can offer and yet it's still not enough. Their heart still has a big hole in it so that whatever they pour into it pours right back out. And as I reach for that goal of being filled, I still remember almost forty years ago when I had it perfect.

The hole that Chris speaks of is the father-shaped hole that is inside each of us. And if it is not filled for us, we will seek to fill it every day of our lives. When we are looking for something to fill that hole, what we are really doing is searching for intimacy, looking for someone who will be a real father to us. Chris found that father in God, his heavenly Father.

Searching for Intimacy

No matter who we are, our hearts cry out for an intimate relationship with a father. If we are deprived of that relationship, we will find something else, however inadequate it may be, to try and fill that emotional hole in our hearts. Many fatherless kids join gangs to get the intimacy they need. The gang serves as a surrogate father, providing companionship, support, and a sense of belonging. Others get involved in sex, hoping to find the intimacy they lack at home. Susan is one example.

If you met Susan on the street, you might think that she sang in her church choir or taught Sunday School. In reality, she has slept with three different men this past week and has been with 12 others over the past month. How did she develop such a lifestyle? Her problem started a long time ago.

At the age of 8 Susan said to herself: *Something must be wrong with me. My daddy won't hug me or touch me or spend time with me. I guess I'm not what I ought to be. If I were, Daddy would love me!*

Her father was a decent man, but he had grown up in a home in which parents did not touch their children to show affection. Such children, as they mature, often relate physical affection to sexual intimacy. Much to the detriment of their children they tend as fathers to be non-touchers.

By the time Susan was 13, she tried to find in other men the love that her father had withheld from her. Her promiscuity caused her to be popular with older boys and even with older men.

She later married, not because she deeply loved her husband but to get the affection she had always wanted but never had received from her father. As you can imagine, the couple had serious problems. After a while, one man could not meet Susan's insatiable desire for affection. Apart from the grace of God, such a marriage had no chance to succeed![2]

Susan made the mistake of equating sexual activity with intimacy. Since she had no intimacy with her father, who never touched her or showed his love for her in any visible way, it was only natural for her to conclude that intimacy meant getting as much touching and physical contact as possible.

Please understand that the intimacy we are talking about in this chapter has nothing to do with sex. Susan may have suffered from a distant and unaffectionate father, but children in many other families have the opposite experience. Unfortunately for many children, particularly daughters, memories of father are memories of being molested, sexually abused, or even raped. To them, the idea of intimacy with a father conjures up images that are extremely painful,

> *Being a father requires more than the capability to produce offspring.*

frightening, and repugnant. No, the intimacy we are talking about is the "full well" intimacy, an emotional connection at the most basic level between father and child, a connection that opens a channel for the free flow of love, affirmation, approval, and emotional nurturing. Sadly, many children today do not have that kind of relationship with their fathers.

In America today we are raising a fatherless generation. Biologically speaking, of course, we *all* have fathers. However, being a *real* father, a *loving* father, an *emotionally supportive* and *affirming* father requires more than just the physiological capability to produce offspring. It requires a fundamental emotional connection with one's children, a connection many fathers today do not have and never have had because their own emotional growth was stunted by negative experiences as children. Consequently, they have never learned to reach out. What they *have* learned is how to put up all kinds of defenses to avoid being hurt again.

As we have already seen, men and women whose fathers were empty wells to them often grow up to be empty wells themselves. Starved of love and intimacy with their fathers, they starve their own children the same way while at the same time becoming obsessed with trying to establish that intimate connection with their fathers that they never had.

Quite often people in this situation settle into lifestyles based on works. Because they have such a crying need for the affirmation and admiration of other people, their self-worth becomes dependent on how well they perform. Their self-esteem rises or falls with the balance sheet, and they are intensely concerned about their own reputation and how they appear to others. The standards they apply to themselves they apply also to others, particularly those in their immediate sphere of influence, such as family, employees, or congregation. From this perspective, these empty wells view other people as commodities whose value is measured on how hard they work, how much they contribute to the organization, and how useful they are in enhancing the empty well's reputation and public standing.

This same drive to perform and work and excel characterizes an empty well's efforts to establish a connection with his or her empty well father. Since there is no healthy relationship upon which to build, something else must provide the foundation. Usually, it is works and, just as usually, works doesn't work.

Cynthia is a single woman who has suffered an abusive relationship with her father. Out of her desire to please him and to get him to love and affirm her the way she needs him to, she tries to make everything per- fect and smooth so as not to upset him. No matter to what lengths she goes to make him happy, it always ends up with him cussing her out and telling her what a disappointment she is. Nevertheless, Cynthia is still trying to please her father, still trying to get from him what he has never given her before and never will give her unless he sees the light and decides to change.

Deep inside, empty wells long for fulfilling relationships.

Empty well people like Cynthia and her father are program- and performance-driven rather than relationship-motivated. Everything they do and every- thing they value centers on working and achieving rather than on loving and being. They have become so starved for a true, fulfilling relationship that they may even develop an outward contempt for such a thing, writing it off as a sign of weakness and deriding it as "mushy, sentimental emotionalism." In real- ity they are extremely envious because deep inside, a fulfill- ing relationship is the very thing they long for most.

Because working and earning and achieving are the only ways they know how to relate to others, they approach God the same way. Generally speaking, empty well people lack an inti- mate relationship with God. Since they have never experienced true intimacy, they have no idea what it really is or any clue how to attain it. A person could be a pastor, a deacon, a lay leader, a Sunday school teacher, a children's worker, a youth minister, a discipleship minister, or even a worship leader and still be an empty well; still have no deep, intimate relationship with God.

Seeking Your Heavenly Father

People who have trouble relating to their earthly fathers usually have trouble relating to God, their heavenly Father. Earthly relationships generally reflect spiritual relationships. If you are a distant, aloof, and cold person who never gets close to anyone else, you will treat God the same way. If you hold a lot of anger or resentment or bitterness toward your earthly father, you will likely be angry, resentful, or bitter toward God. On the other hand, if you have a warm, loving, open, sharing, and caring relationship with your earthly father, you will probably feel the same way about God.

Your earthly father relationship reflects your heavenly Father relationship.

What's the status of your relationship with your earthly father? Good? Bad? Non-existent? Angry? Hateful? Resentful? Bitter? Empty? Warm? Open? Loving? Friendly? Perhaps your father is no longer living. How did the two of you get along when he was still alive?

Maybe you never knew your father. He may have died before you were born or abandoned you early on, leaving you and your mom alone, perhaps with brothers and sisters. How do you feel about a man you have never known? What emotions do you associate with this shadowy, unknown figure from your past?

Maybe your father abused you either verbally or sexually. Maybe he beat you. Maybe he belittled you every chance he got. Maybe he simply ignored you, causing you to feel invisible every time you were near him. Maybe he was like Susan's father and never touched you or showed any visible signs of love or affection for you. What feelings arise in your heart when you hear the word *father*?

No matter where your relationship with your earthly father stands, you *can* have a rich, fulfilling, and nourishing relationship with your heavenly Father. It doesn't matter how old you are, how well or how poorly you get along with your earthly dad, or how long you have been struggling in the arid desert of the empty well syndrome. Recognizing the love of God in your life will turn your whole situation around.

This kind of goes back to what we talked about in Chapter One, but it bears repeating: *God loves you and seeks an intimate love relationship with you.* That may sound simply too good to be true to some of you, but take it from me, it *is* true. The entire Bible from Genesis to Revelation is the story of God at work restoring our severed relationship with Him. He wants to be more to us than just the Creator and the King of kings; He wants to be our *Father.*

Even if you have the best father on earth, God can be everything your earthly father is or was, and *more.* If your earthly father was abusive, absent, inattentive, cold, violent, or whatever, God can be for you everything your earthly father was *not*. Whatever you needed from your earthly father but never got, God can give you. He wants to be your Father.

If you want to know what kind of Father-child relationship you can have with God, just take a look at the relationship Jesus had with His Father: perfect intimacy, perfect harmony, perfect fellowship, perfect love. Jesus' life on earth demonstrated what Adam and Eve's relationship with God *should* have been (and was before they sinned), and what ours can be again in Him. Listen to some of the ways Jesus described His relationship with His Father:

God wants to be your Father.

I and the Father are one (John 10:30).

Believe me when I say that I am in the Father and the Father is in me (John 14:11a).

The world must learn that I love the Father and that I do exactly what my Father has commanded me (John 14:31).

I am the true vine, and my Father is the gardener (John 15:1).

As the Father has loved me, so have I loved you. Now remain in my love. If you obey my commands, you will remain in my love, just as I have obeyed my Father's commands and remain in his love (John 15:9-10).

...Father, the time has come. Glorify your Son, that your Son may glorify you....I have brought you glory

on earth by completing the work you gave me to do. And now, Father, glorify me in your presence with the glory I had with you before the world began (John 17:1, 4-5).

Every one of these verses reveals perfect intimacy that Jesus had with His Father—an intimacy that is available to us as well. Consider what Jesus has to say about our relationship with our heavenly Father:

But when you pray, go into your room, close the door and pray to your Father, who is unseen. Then your Father, who sees what is done in secret, will reward you (Matthew 6:6).

So do not worry, saying, "What shall we eat?" or "What shall we drink?" or "What shall we wear?" For the pagans run after all these things, and your heavenly Father knows that you need them. But seek first his kingdom and his righteousness, and all these things will be given to you as well (Matthew 6:31-33).

Ask and it will be given to you; seek and you will find; knock and the door will be opened to you. For everyone who asks receives; he who seeks finds; and to him who knocks, the door will be opened (Matthew 7:7-8).

Do not be afraid, little flock, for your Father has been pleased to give you the kingdom (Luke 12:32).

God wants to be our Father. He wants to have an intimate love relationship with each of us. In His infinite divine wisdom, He placed inside each of us a "Father hunger" that is designed to lead us to Him. He instituted the family with father and mother to guide their children and point the way. Unfortunately, sin corrupted and distorted the picture. Because of sin, we are all corrupt and flawed. No one is perfect. Nobody has ever had perfect parents or perfect children and nobody ever will. No other human being will ever be able to provide us with everything we need with perfect consistency. Only God can do that.

God loves you with a perfect love. Whatever you are lacking, whatever your earthly father or mother or other caregiver could not give you, God can supply. You have a Father, a heavenly Father, and a Father makes all the difference.

Endnotes

1. Robert S. McGee, Pat Springle, and Jim Craddock, *Breaking the Cycle of Hurtful Family Experiences* (Nashville: Lifeway Press of Lifeway Christian Resources; c. 1994 by Rapha Publishing, Houston, TX, Reprint 2001), p. 9.

2. Ibid, pp. 20-21.

Chapter Eight

NO MORE BEGGING

Bartimaeus' keen ears detected the sound of the crowd long before it reached the city gate. Jericho was usually bustling anyway, but today even more so. Judging from the noise level, a sizeable throng of people was making its way through the city. From his place by the roadside just beyond the gate, Bartimaeus could hear an excited babble of voices as the crowd approached. It seemed as though everyone was trying to talk at once. What was going on? Was some important dignitary passing through town? Who could stir up the people so? Something unusual definitely was happening in Jericho today. Bartimaeus pulled his beggar's cloak more tightly around himself and held up his alms bowl in anticipation.

As the first of the crowd began pouring through the gate, Bartimaeus' sharp ears picked up snatches of conversation here and there, along with a distinctive accent he recognized from years of begging by the roadside. A Galilean accent. At least some in the crowd were from Galilee in the far north. In the midst of all the excitement and confusion, Bartimaeus added his own voice to the clamor, turning his white, sightless eyes upward and calling out in a loud voice, "Alms for the blind! Alms for the blind! Have mercy on a blind man! Alms for the blind!"

Immediately he heard the satisfying clink as first one coin, then another, then another clattered into his uplifted alms bowl. This would be a good day for a blind beggar!

All around him the frenzied atmosphere intensified. People were laughing, shouting, and calling out to one another and to someone in the midst of the crowd. Bartimaeus kept hearing the name *Jesus* on the lips of the people. Then he caught the word *Nazareth*.

Jesus of Nazareth? Bartimaeus was stunned. The healer from Galilee? Bartimaeus had heard the news of the young carpenter from Nazareth who went around preaching and teaching and healing people. A blind beggar by the roadside heard a lot of things as travelers came and went. But Jesus? Here in Jericho? Could it really be? Bartimaeus had never expected to meet Jesus, and now he was about to lose what might be his only opportunity!

Letting his alms bowl fall to the ground, Bartimaeus lifted his arms in the air and cried out with a louder voice than before, "Jesus! Son of David! Have mercy on me! Jesus! Son of David! Have mercy on me!" Bystanders near him began to rebuke him. One even cuffed his ear and said, "Shut up, you fool! He doesn't have time for the likes of you!"

Ignoring the insult, Bartimaeus kept shouting, "Jesus! Son of David! Have mercy on me! Jesus! Son of David! Have mercy on me!" Gradually the hubbub subsided until the crowd was strangely quiet. Then Bartimaeus heard a calm, gentle voice say, "Call him."

Someone tapped Bartimaeus on the shoulder and a voice—a different, kinder voice this time—said, "Cheer up! Get on your feet! He's calling for you!" Bartimaeus scrambled to his feet, letting his beggar's cloak slide to the ground. The same kind person who had spoken to him now took his arm and guided him to Jesus. As Bartimaeus stood there, trembling slightly in excitement and anticipation, the same calm, gentle voice that had said, "Call him," spoke again.

"What do you want Me to do for you?"

"Rabbi," Bartimaeus blurted out desperately, "I want to see!"

"Go," Jesus replied. "Your faith has healed you."

Instantly, light flooded Bartimaeus' eyes. Shapes and images came into sharp focus. Colors brighter and sharper and more varied than he had ever imagined! Glorious blue sky! Bright sunshine! Faces all around him, some smiling, some in shocked amazement. Then his new-seeing eyes became riveted on one face—the smiling, compassionate face of Jesus, the One who had given him his sight. Placing His hand on the shoulder of the once-blind man, Jesus broke into laughter, sharing in Bartimaeus' joy.

Jesus then turned and continued on His way. Bartimaeus, his beggar's cloak and alms bowl forgotten in the dust of the roadside, fell in with the crowd and followed Jesus down the road.[1]

From Rags to Riches

When blind beggar Bartimaeus met Jesus, his life changed forever. Not only did he receive his sight, but he also was ushered into a richer, fuller, and more complete life than he could ever have imagined. Once he saw Jesus—once he knew Jesus—Bartimaeus also knew that his days as a beggar were gone forever. Oh sure, there would be trials and difficulties ahead—following Jesus always guarantees tribulation—

When we know God as Father, our whole lives change.

but now Bartimaeus would face whatever came along not as a penniless, powerless beggar, a cast-off of society, an "invisible man" considered cursed by God because of his blindness, but as a redeemed child of God, his heavenly Father. In one brilliant instant, Bartimaeus was transformed from rags to riches, from sinner to saint, from a pauper of the land to a prince in his Father's house.

In our own way, we are all like Bartimaeus. We may not be physically blind or living in poverty, but we are all beggars nonetheless. Sin has separated us from God, our Father, and from our rightful place as children in His house. No matter who we are or how successful we are in the eyes of the world; no matter how much money or status we possess, apart from the forgiving, saving power of Christ, we are nothing more than paupers, helpless and hopeless next to the holiness and righteousness of God and His kingdom.

Also, like Bartimaeus, once we come to know God as our Father through faith in Jesus Christ, our whole live change. With God as our Father, we become children of the King. He transforms us from darkness to light, from blindness to sight, from rags to riches, and from abandoned orphans to beloved sons and daughters. He lifts us up as penniless paupers and makes us into princes and princesses of God.

When God chose a people to be His very own, He began with Abraham, promising him a land that would belong to him and to his descendants forever. God also promised Abraham a son from whom a great nation, a chosen nation, would descend. From this chosen nation someday would come the Messiah, the "Anointed One," who would save His people—and all the people of the earth—from their sins.

To Abraham was born Isaac, who later had two sons of his own: Jacob and Esau. It was Jacob's descendants who would become the great nation that God had promised to Abraham. Jacob's name means "supplanter," or "trickster," one who grabs the heel of another to trip him up, just as Jacob was born grasping the heel of his twin brother, Esau. I guess you could say that Jacob was a beggar, too. He certainly lived up to his name, deceiving and scheming and grasping with the best of them until the day he came face to face with his own destiny. Behind him lay 21 years of hard labor in his uncle's fields, during which time he acquired two wives, two concubines, 11 sons, and a great wealth of sheep, goats, cattle, camels, and donkeys. Ahead of him lay a meeting with his brother Esau, who had once sworn to kill him.

Sending his family and flocks and herds and servants ahead of him, Jacob remained alone and all that night wrestled with God in the form of a "man" who appeared to him in the night. After this encounter, Jacob received a new name, Israel, which means "he strives with God," or "prince of God." This name also became the name of the nation that grew out of Jacob and his sons. Israel, the chosen people of God, was a nation of "princes" of God.

The New Testament makes it clear that all who follow Jesus are included as a part of the "true" Israel, spiritual Israel, who are the true heirs of God and His kingdom. In his letter to the Romans, the apostle Paul went to great lengths to explain this, saying in part:

> For I could wish that I myself were cursed and cut off from Christ for the sake of my brothers, those of my own race, the people of Israel. Theirs is the adoption as sons; theirs the divine glory, the covenants, the receiving of the law, the temple worship and the promises. Theirs are the patriarchs, and from them is traced the human ancestry of Christ, who is God over all, forever praised! Amen. It is not as though God's word had failed. For not all who are descended from Israel are Israel. Nor because they are his descendants are they all Abraham's children. On the contrary, "It is through Isaac that your offspring will be reckoned." In other words, it is not the natural children who are God's children, but it is the children of the promise who are regarded as Abraham's offspring (Romans 9:3-8).

Stated simply, true "Israel," the true "princes of God," are *all* people, regardless of race or gender, who, like Abraham, are children of faith in God through Jesus Christ. All who know and follow Christ are heirs of God's promise to Israel. Paul stated this unequivocally in Ephesians:

> This mystery is that through the gospel the Gentiles are heirs together with Israel, members together of one body, and sharers together in the promise in Christ Jesus (Ephesians 3:6).

No More Begging

It is a true rags to riches story, as Peter pointed out:

But you are a chosen people, a royal priesthood, a holy nation, a people belonging to God, that you may declare the praises of him who called you out of darkness into his wonderful light. Once you were not a people, but now you are the people of God; once you had not received mercy, but now you have received mercy (1 Peter 2:9-10).

What does this mean for us? Very simply, it means that once we know God as our Father through faith in Jesus Christ our Lord, we become part of "true Israel"; we become princes and princesses of God. In other words, we are the King's kids!

Children of the King don't beg!

The King's children don't go around begging for scraps from the table. They don't go around begging for attention. They don't wear rags or hand-me-down clothes. They don't have to work to earn their status. They are part of the family, heirs of their Father, the King. Everything that belongs to the King belongs to them.

Once we know God as our Father, we become His children, heirs of His kingdom and of all that belongs to Him. *We are not beggars anymore!*

Act Like Who You Really Are

If we are not beggars anymore, then why do so many of us act as though we are? At least part of the answer lies in the fact that even though we are now children of God, we have not yet learned to think like children of God. Our minds are still oriented to a beggar's point of view. This is especially true for those of us with the empty well syndrome. After all, it's only natural. All our lives we have been begging in one form or another—begging for love, begging for attention, begging for recognition, begging for admiration, begging for intimacy—until begging has become an entrenched way of life, so embedded in our lifestyles that we no longer even realize that we are doing it. Begging has been a part of us for so long that we cannot even conceive of any other way to live.

We have begged for so long that we can't imagine not begging.

When you hear the word *beggar*, what image comes to mind? A homeless person sleeping on a park bench? Some down-on-his-luck character who just lost his job and hits you up for a couple of bucks? A drunk passed out in the gutter? A junkie shooting up in a crack house? A disheveled woman in mismatched clothes and worn-out shoes pushing her meager belongings in front of her in an old rattling shopping cart? A blind man peddling pencils or newspapers on the street corner? Kids with rubber squeegees who clean your windshield at a traffic light and then put their hands out for a quarter?

Stereotypes? Some of them, perhaps, but even stereotypes have a basis in reality; otherwise they wouldn't *be* stereotypes. Beggars come in all sorts of disguises and pop up in places we would never dream of finding them. What about the man in the three-piece suit sitting in his high-rise office scheming to steal his boss's job? The pastor who will never be happy until his church has more members than any other church in town? The class clown who always has to be the center of attention? The supervisor who throws her weight around because she can and wants everybody to know it? The young woman who gets into one dead-end sexual relationship after another? The corporate CEO who is cutting corners and employee benefits to increase his own profit margin? Corporate executives who use insider trading tips to enrich themselves at shareholders' and employees' expense? A parent who dangles love or approval before a child (whatever the age) as a "carrot" to control that child's actions? A child (whatever the age) who continually sacrifices his or her own dreams or desires or plans to go after the dangled carrot?

All of these are beggars too because they all display one common characteristic of beggars: *dependency*. Whether it is cutthroat corporate ambition, the need to be admired and respected by others, the need to feel important, the hunger for affection, greed, an obsession with control, or an overpowering desire to please, someone or something controls each of these people so that their lives are not their own. Believing themselves to be free agents, they are in fact bound by that which controls and drives them to seek what they seek and to do what they do.

Lack of freedom is another characteristic of beggars. Beggars are never free but are bound by their circumstances. The old adage "beggars can't be choosers" contains a lot of truth. For beggars there is little choice; theirs is a "take it or leave it" situation.

Children of the King, on the other hand, are not beggars. They are free to choose, to chart their own courses, to follow their own dreams, and to realize their full potential. All options are open to them because the unlimited resources of their Father, the King, are at their disposal.

What about you? Are you a beggar? Or are you a King's kid? Even if you *are* a King's kid, as long as you continue to think like a beggar, you will continue to act like a beggar.

"Okay, Mark," you may ask, "maybe I do think like a beggar, but how do I know? How can I tell?"

Take some time to look deep inside yourself. Ask yourself some questions. Do any of these ring true for you?

Is your happiness, contentment, or sense of well-being or self-worth dependent on someone else's opinion of you or on your ability to keep that person happy? Does life often make you feel as though you are sitting in the dust outside the gate while everyone else is inside enjoying an elegant banquet? Do certain people in your life make you feel invisible around them? Do you feel powerless to change your circumstances? Are you still working to earn someone's love or approval? Are you living for someone else's dreams instead of your own? Do you continually sacrifice your own happiness in a vain attempt to please somebody else? Do you continually tailor your schedule and plans around another's expectations? Have you bought into someone's constant criticism of you and begun to believe it yourself? Do you allow that person to constantly "push your buttons"? Do you find yourself surrendering control to him or her—again and again? Are you killing yourself over a career? Are you killing yourself trying to get a bigger house, a bigger car, a bigger paycheck, a bigger bank account, a bigger reputation?

If any of these struck a responsive chord in your spirit—if you answered "yes" to any of them—then you are still thinking like a beggar, at least to some degree. A beggar mentality is based on works. It says, "Nothing is free. To get anywhere, to be somebody, you have to work, work, work and push, push, push." Success is measured by how big you are, how rich you are, by the car you drive, by the house you live in, by how many people know your name, by how many people you have under you, by how much power you have, and by how much influence you exert.

Are you a beggar or are you a King's kid? A beggar's mentality is what keeps you locked in your empty well situation. Even if you are a child of God, as long as you allow some other person or situation or circumstance to control the way you live, you will never experience freedom. It's time to say "bye-bye" to beggarly thinking and to trade it in for a new way of thinking, a "King's kid" mentality based not on works but on grace. It's time to stop acting like a beggar and to start acting like who you really are—a King's kid.

> *A beggar mentality is based on works.*

By Grace, Not By Works

A King's kid mentality is based on grace. It says, "Everything is free. You don't have to beg anymore. You don't have to work to become somebody because you already *are* somebody. You're a child of the King. You don't have to beg for love because your Father already loves you with an infinite love. You don't have to beg for attention because your Father's delighted eyes are always on you and His attentive ear is never more than a prayer away. You don't have to beg for approval because your Father already approves of you completely. You don't have to beg for acceptance because your Father has already accepted you on the basis of His Son's death for the forgiveness of your sins. You don't have to beg for affirmation because your Father has given His Spirit to live inside you to encourage you, to teach you, to guide you, and to help you in the way you should go."

God shows us favor because He wants to.

One reason so many of us who are children of God have so much trouble giving up our beggar's mentality is because we have such a poor understanding of the grace of God. The word *grace* means "unmerited favor." God shows favor toward us not because we deserve it (we don't) but because He wants to. Grace is God's free gift to us; free to us but enormously costly to Him. The price God paid to give us grace was the blood of His own Son. No higher price could ever be paid; no costlier gift could ever be given. That is why no begging is necessary; why no "works" will work. The highest price has already been paid; nothing we could ever do could ever add any value to that price. Grace is grace; there is no such thing as "value-added" grace.

Even so, we in our pride want to insist that there *must* be something that we have to do. Steeped as we are in the beggar's mentality that says there is no such thing as a free lunch, the idea of such a free gift from God sounds too good to be true. Nevertheless, it is true. Nowhere does the Bible say that we have to beg for our Father's love, attention, favor, or anything else from His hand. In fact, the Bible teaches the exact opposite. Everything God does toward us is an act of His grace because otherwise we could never receive it. The apostle Paul spoke of grace often. It was one of his primary themes:

For it is by grace you have been saved, through faith— and this not from yourselves, it is the gift of God—not by works, so that no one can boast (Ephesians 2:8-9).

For all have sinned and fall short of the glory of God, and are justified freely by his grace through the redemption that came by Christ Jesus (Romans 3:23-24).

Therefore, the promise comes by faith, so that it may be by grace and may be guaranteed to all Abraham's offspring—not only to those who are of the law but also to those who are of the faith of Abraham. He is the father of us all (Romans 4:16).

Therefore, since we have been justified through faith, we have peace with God through our Lord Jesus Christ, through whom we have gained access by faith into this grace in which we now stand. And we rejoice in the hope of the glory of God (Romans 5:1-2).

For sin shall not be your master, because you are not under law, but under grace (Romans 6:14).

I have been crucified with Christ and I no longer live, but Christ lives in me. The life I live in the body, I live by faith in the Son of God, who loved me and gave himself for me. I do not set aside the grace of God, for if righteousness could be gained through the law, Christ died for nothing! (Galatians 2:20-21)

[God] has saved us and called us to a holy life—not because of anything we have done but because of his

*own purpose and grace. This grace was given us in Christ
Jesus before the beginning of time* (2 Timothy 1:9).

Everything we will ever need from our Father—everything
we have been searching for and begging for and working for
all our lives—He has already given us in abundant measure by
His grace. Once we believe and understand the truth and
power of God's grace extended to us, our whole mentality will
change. Our old beggarly way of thinking will be gone forever. In its place will be the mentality of children of the King, a
mind-set of freedom and wholeness where the sky is the limit.
Grace means *no more begging.*

Pathway to Freedom

Once you have realized that you have been going to an
empty well all these years or that you have been an empty
well; once you have decided to change no matter what; once
you have determined that you will not be an empty well for
your family and others who rely on you; once you have taken
back control of your life by giving it to Christ; once you have
forgiven your empty well and let him or her off the hook; once
you have come to a solid understanding that you have a heavenly Father who is to you everything you will ever need—then
you are ready to take your first steps toward a freedom you
have never known before.

No more begging; you are free. No longer do you need to
go back to that empty well over and over because now you
are learning to find what you need elsewhere. No more begging for scraps of love, morsels of affection, or crumbs of
affirmation. You have found a place where you can receive all
of these in abundance. No more indentured servitude to the

desires and expectations of your empty well. No more submitting yourself to live someone else's life or fulfill someone else's dreams. You are free now to live your own life.

You've come a long way since your journey began, but it's not over yet. There comes a time when you have to actually make the break with your empty well. How you make the break will depend on your personality and the personality of your empty well, as well as on the particular situation you are in. It may come with a face-to-face conversation and a possible blowup, or you may make the break quietly, subtly adjusting your attitude and acknowledging new boundaries and parameters in your relationship that remove your emotional dependency on the person who has failed to fill you all these years.

> *You are free now to live your own life.*

The stakes are high. It affects not only your own spiritual and emotional welfare, but also that of your family, as well as the chance to break the cycle of the empty well syndrome in your generation so you do not pass it on to your children.

Whether in direct, honest dialogue, or only in your own mind, you have to reach the place where you can say:

> "If I can't have your attention, then I'm sorry, but I have to go. I'm not going to get into a conversation that talks only about you anymore because it is not a mutual relationship. A true relationship is mutually beneficial: I give something and you give something. If you're interested only in talking about yourself and your needs, well, I need to move on.

"I'm not going to beg for your attention anymore because I know that you have nothing to give me. Until you come to the place in *your* life where you are willing to become a full well, our relationship is at its peak. I have chosen to change; until you choose to change, our relationship can go no further.

"I'm not going to kill myself for your attention anymore. I'm not going to go beyond the call of duty anymore, even though it is my innate nature to want to please you. No longer will I sacrifice my own needs just to get your attention."

If this sounds harsh, keep in mind that making a break like this is almost always painful, but sometimes a radical or even drastic step is called for. Let me stress again, however, that this is a breaking of an emotional dependency, *not* an abandonment of your empty well. This does *not* mean leaving your spouse for someone else. It does *not* mean shutting your parents or your children out of your life. It does *not* mean having nothing more to do with the person whose dependency you are freeing yourself from.

It *does* mean acknowledging the emotional limitations of your relationship. It *does* mean freeing yourself from depending on them for something they cannot give. It *does* mean freeing them to be who they are. It *does* mean going to them for what they *can* give, but no longer holding them responsible for what they *cannot* give.

One sign of real healing and transformation is when you can decide on occasion to go "beyond the call of duty" again for your empty well, not out of a desire to please or to get attention or to fill a need in your life, but simply out of love for your empty well and a desire to pour into that person the love you never received. You're not looking to get anything back, but are giving as an expression of your love. In other words, you go back to your empty well not to get something out but to put something in with no expectations and no strings attached. *That, my friends, is freedom.*

Don't Forget Where You Came From

All of us who are in Christ and have God as our Father are former beggars. Now we are royal children who sit at the King's table enjoying His abundant feast. But how can we do nothing else but sit at the table while there are other beggars outside the gate who need to be brought inside as we were? Now that we are no longer beggars, but free children in our Father's house, we need to go outside and bring our fellow beggars in so that they can become free as well. We have been set free, but in our freedom, let us never forget where we came from.

> *In our freedom, let us never forget where we came from.*

Now that we have God as our Father, we no longer need to beg for attention or for love or for affirmation because He gives us all of those that we will ever need. As His love, attention, and affirmation flow into us, we can become open channels, full wells, access points through which they can flow to others.

Around midnight on March 29, 1848, the mighty cataracts of Niagara Falls stopped flowing. For 30 to 40 hours the "falls" were dry as lake ice from Lake Erie many miles upstream jammed the Niagara River, stopping its flow. Once the ice cleared, the river began to flow again and the falls returned to normal.

Like Niagara Falls, the flow of *our* water can get jammed up also by sin, anger, bitterness, hurt, resentment, an unforgiving spirit, etc. When we learn to let God's water flow into and through us, that "ice jam" of human emotional debris that is shutting off our flow is cleaned out. Instead of a jammed-up stream, we become a full-flowing river; instead of a trickling, brackish spring, we become a deep well of cool, clear, refreshing, life-giving water.

Once you were a beggar; now you are a child of the King. Once you were bound; now you are free. Once you were a jammed-up stream; now you are an open well. Don't forget where you came from. Let your water flow!

Endnote

1. See Mark 10:46-52.

Chapter Nine

DRINK FROM THE
LIVING WATER

If you're going to let your water flow, make sure you are drawing from the right source.

Imagine that you have just purchased a brand-new house in a nice new subdivision; it's the home of your dreams. On the day the moving van is scheduled to deliver all your household goods, you arrive at the house a couple of hours early just to walk through the rooms. The floor coverings, the color schemes, the draperies, the trim—everything is exactly as you ordered it. The windows are clean and new, the paint fresh and sparkling. The kitchen and bathroom fixtures gleam. Everything is perfect.

Thirsty, you go into the kitchen to get a drink of water. Imagine your horror when you turn on the tap in the sink and instead of cool, clear water, raw sewage comes out! The plumbing contractor has made a colossal mistake and hooked up the water pipes to the sewer line instead of the water main! Your new home, regardless of its outward beauty and perfection, is uninhabitable until extensive and expensive corrections are made. You simply cannot live there until the water is flowing.

You simply cannot live without a flow of water.

It is so easy to take a dependable source of clean water for granted, especially if you have lived in the city all your life.

Mike and Debbie just bought a house in the mountains. After years of city living, their dream of a quiet country hideaway has finally come true. Because their new home is on top of a mountain several miles from the nearest community, it has a self-contained water system. A well may lie in the future for their property, but for now Mike and Debbie's house is equipped with a cistern—two large tanks and a smaller auxiliary tank. Although the cistern is set up to capture rainwater runoff, that alone does not supply all of their water needs. In addition, every few weeks they have water delivered and pumped into the tanks by a water hauling service.

Switching from city water to a self-contained system was quite an adjustment for Mike and Debbie. Because they moved in during the winter, they learned very quickly not to take their water for granted. Twice during their first week in the house, their water pump froze, leaving them with no water pressure. No pressure, no water. After thawing the pump they were okay for a few days until the water stopped again. This time, they discovered the cistern was empty. Upon moving in, they had assumed erroneously that the tanks had already been filled. They called for a water delivery, then had a special float system installed in the cistern to warn them when the water level is low so they won't run out again.

One day, immediately after receiving a supply of water, Mike and Debbie discovered once again that no water was flowing into the house. The problem this time was clogged filters. Because of the rainwater collection setup, their water system uses two sediment filters to filter out dirt and sediment so that the water flowing into the house is always clean. Water pouring into the tanks during delivery had stirred up sediment at the bottom of the tanks, causing the filters to become clogged. After changing the filters, Mike and Debbie have decided that in the future they will shut off the water line into the house during water delivery so that the sediment will have time to settle without being pumped into the line to clog the filters again.

Despite all these little "adventures," Mike and Debbie love their new house. Gradually, through trial and error, these "city folk" are learning country ways. Most of all, they have learned not to take their water for granted. It is a precious commodity for which they have developed a whole new appreciation.

Find a New Well

Nothing is more important than having access to a dependable supply of water. Water sustains human life. Without it, we will die in as little as three days.

A steady supply of emotional "water" is just as important in sustaining our spirits. Your emotional needs are legitimate and too important to ignore. If the well you have been drinking from no longer fills or satisfies you, find another one. It is not enough simply to break your emotional dependency on a person who is an empty well to you. Because your need is still there, you need to find another well, a full well, someone who will feed into your life in a way your empty well cannot.

It could be just about anyone. If one of your parents is an empty well for you, your other parent may be the person you need. A grandfather or grandmother, a son or a daughter, a close friend, a pastor or a Sunday school teacher, even a co-worker—any of these may prove to be a full well for you to draw from, a person whose spirit will feed your spirit and nourish your life in a way nobody else can.

Myrna became interested in quilting as a young woman while she was laid up in bed recovering from major surgery. Cutting quilting squares and hand-stitching them together was an activity she could do without getting out of bed. Since taking up her new pastime, Myrna has displayed quite a talent for making quilts and revealed a remarkable eye for colors and balance. She has tried to interest her parents in her hobby, even once excitedly showing them her latest finished quilt. To her extreme disappointment, her architect father and CPA mother were unimpressed. They even went as far as to tell her that she was wasting her time with "frivolous pursuits" and should do something worthwhile with her life. It was the same type of thing Myrna has always heard from her parents.

Recently, Myrna discovered that her maternal grandmother is also a quilt maker. Now Myrna visits her grandmother several times a week and they have started to get together regularly to do quilting. This is more than just a shared hobby, for when they are together they talk about life and love and about Myrna's hopes and dreams and plans for the future. Myrna cherishes these times and eagerly anticipates her next visit. For Myrna, her grandmother is a store of wisdom and gentle love, a refreshing draught for her thirsty heart. Myrna has found in her grandmother a new well, a full well to satisfy her deepest longing.

When searching for a new well, look for someone with a kindred spirit. This may prove to be more intuitive than conscious. When two people "connect" emotionally on a particular level, there is a certain "knowingness" that occurs in their hearts, drawing them together.

Look for someone with a kindred spirit to be your new well.

Use prudence and discretion, however, because looks can be deceiving. Not everyone who appears to be a full well is a full well. It depends on the source of their water. Remember, a well is not the source of the water, but an access point to the water. The water may be good or it may be bad, so be careful about the well you choose. What good is a full well if it contains nothing but foul, brackish, stagnant water? Make sure that the well you choose is connected to the right source: clean, pure, life-giving water. *Living water.*

Jesus Is the Living Water

As we noted in Chapter One, the Bible frequently uses water as a symbol for life. Revelation 22:1-2 speaks of the *"river of the water of life"* that flows from God's throne and nourishes the *"tree of life"* whose leaves provide *"healing of the nations."* Ezekiel chapter 47 also depicts a river flowing from *"under the threshold of the temple"* (verse 1) and inundating the land with a life-giving flood so that *"where the river flows everything will live"* (verse 9).

The Gospel of John identifies Jesus as the source of "living water," thus identifying Him as the source of life. Since only God can give life, this was another way of revealing Jesus' nature as the divine Son of God. The phrase *living water* occurs three times in the Gospel of John, each time associated with Jesus. One instance occurs in connection with the Jewish Feast of Tabernacles:

> *On the last and greatest day of the Feast, Jesus stood and said in a loud voice, "If anyone is thirsty, let him come to me and drink. Whoever believes in me, as the Scripture has said, streams of living water will flow from within him." By this he meant the Spirit, whom those who believed in him were later to receive. Up to that time the Spirit had not been given, since Jesus had not yet been glorified* (John 7:37-39).

The Feast of Tabernacles, a weeklong festival when the people lived for a week in booths or lean-tos made from tree branches, commemorated the ingathering of the harvest as well as the time when the people of Israel lived in such booths after their exodus from Egypt. One later addition to the festival that was well in place by Jesus' day was a ritual in which every day a libation of water from the pool of Siloam was taken in solemn procession to the temple and poured out on the great altar. On the last day of the festival, this ritual was marked by a special water-pouring rite and lights ceremony. A common belief grew up over the years that when the Messiah appeared, He would reveal Himself at this festival during this ritual.

Jesus did reveal Himself at that time and place, but His own people did not receive Him. He offered *"living water"* to anyone who was thirsty. This living water was His life-giving Spirit.

The other references in John to "living water" occur in connection with a conversation Jesus had with a Samaritan woman at a well in the village of Sychar. It was about noon. Jesus' disciples had gone into the village to buy food, so Jesus was alone and resting by the well.

> When a Samaritan woman came to draw water, Jesus said to her, "Will you give me a drink?"…The Samaritan woman said to him, "You are a Jew and I am a Samaritan woman. How can you ask me for a drink?" (For Jews do not associate with Samaritans.) Jesus answered her, "If you knew the gift of God and who it is that asks you for a drink, you would have asked him and he would have given you living water." "Sir," the woman said, "you have nothing to draw with and the well is deep. Where can you get this living water? Are you greater than our father Jacob, who gave us the well and drank from it himself, as did also his sons and his flocks and herds?" Jesus answered, "Everyone who drinks this water will be thirsty again, but whoever drinks the water I give him will never thirst. Indeed, the water I give him will become in him a spring of water welling up to eternal life" (John 4:7, 9-14).

Beginning with a simple question, a request for water, Jesus initiates a dialogue with this Samaritan woman. That in itself was unusual for a couple of reasons. First, it was not customary in that day for a man and woman who were neither married nor related to talk in public. Second, because of severe racial and religious prejudice, Jews and Samaritans normally did not associate with each other, as verse 9 indicates. The woman's reply reveals that she was surprised by Jesus' words and recognized His breach of custom. Nevertheless, it got her talking, and Jesus was able to turn the conversation from a request for literal water to an offer of living water. Jesus offered her a kind of water that would quench her thirst forever and become in her *"a spring of water welling up to eternal life."* The living water Jesus offers goes far beyond the capabilities of natural water. Natural water quenches physical thirst for a time; living water quenches spiritual thirst for eternity.

Living water quenches spiritual thirst for eternity.

The woman was a little slow in understanding what Jesus meant because she next asked for that living water so she would not have to come back to the well and draw water anymore. She was still thinking in terms of literal water. Jesus helped her get her thinking on a spiritual plane by revealing details of her personal life that He could not possibly have known unless He was more than whom He appeared to be. After revealing His knowledge that she had been married five times and was now living with a man who was not her husband, the woman said, "Oh, You must be a prophet" (my paraphrase of verse 19). She then asked a question about religion and proper religious worship. Maybe she was trying to steer the conversation away from the touchy subject of her moral life. At any rate, Jesus engaged her in conversation not only about religion and the "proper" place to worship God, but also about the nature of true worship itself, saying at last, *"God is spirit, and his worshipers must worship in spirit and in truth"* (John 4:24).

The woman, perhaps feeling the futility of "arguing religion," said, *"I know that Messiah (called Christ) is coming. When he comes, he will explain everything to us"* (John 4:25). It sounds like she was dismissing the whole subject by saying, in effect, "Oh, well, we don't have to worry about that right now. When Messiah comes, He'll straighten everything out." That's when Jesus dropped His bombshell: *"I who speak to you am he"* (John 4:26).

Wow! That got her attention! She dropped her water jar, ran back into town, and called all the people in Sychar together—people who normally would not give her the time of day because of her reputation—and said, *"Come, see a man who told me everything I ever did. Could this be the Christ?"* (John 4:29) I believe her question was not out of a desire to know— she already knew Jesus was the Christ, the Messiah—but an expression of faith, almost as if she was saying, "I know He is the Messiah, but it sounds too good to be true!"

At noon on that long-ago day, a Samaritan woman in Sychar went out to get a jar of water from the town well. Instead of returning with just that water, she came back into town with a spring of living water welling up in her to eternal life. Her body would get thirsty again, but not her spirit. She had found what she had been looking for all her life. She had found Jesus, her Messiah, the One who gives living water. She had found her full well, a well that would never run dry, a well that would nourish her spirit forever.

Be Careful Who You Draw Water From

Like the Samaritan woman of Sychar, we all need to learn to drink from the well of living water that Jesus provides. Our primary source of that water is the Holy Spirit who dwells in the life of every believer. The Spirit gives us life, teaches us the ways of God, reveals to us the will of God, and reminds us of everything that Jesus taught. Our human spirits can commune with Christ's Spirit and be completely content, filled, and satisfied.

There is more involved with our lives on earth, however. As long as our spirits inhabit this flesh that we call our bodies, we have connections with other people around us. It is so easy sometimes to get so fixated on attaching ourselves to Jesus that we unconsciously begin to isolate ourselves from interaction with other people, including other believers. That's when we run the risk of becoming "so heavenly minded that we're no earthly good."

Growth does not occur in a vacuum. We humans are not designed to go solo through life. We need each other, and that is just as true for Christians as for anybody else. Jesus may be our living water, but we still need to find and attach ourselves to flesh-and-blood wells who will help us tap into His living water on a regular basis. Many wells are better than one well, just as many perspectives are better than one perspective. Proverbs 15:22 says, *"Plans fail for lack of counsel, but with many advisers they succeed."* The more perspectives we can get the better; the more insights we can receive from other people's viewpoints, the more able we will be to evaluate our own insights to make sure they are correct. We draw strength from one another. As it says in Ecclesiastes, *"Though one may be overpowered, two can defend themselves. A cord of three strands is not quickly broken"* (Ecclesiastes 4:12).

Drink From the Living Water

For this reason, we each need to attach ourselves to a place where we can have an access point to the living water as well as interaction with others seeking the same thing. I'm talking about a Bible-believing, Bible-preaching, and Bible-teaching church with a godly pastor and leadership, both lay and staff. Such a church should have a good balance between teaching and ministry. In other words, the preaching of the Gospel and the teaching of the Word of God should translate into practical, hands-on ministry and service to others.

Be careful who you attach yourself to, however, because not everyone who *says*, "We have living water," actually *has* living water. There are a lot of water vendors out there. Many are solid and legitimate, where you can get a healthy filling every time. Many others are questionable, even downright wrong and dangerous, nothing more than religious snake oil salesmen whose outrageous "cure-all" claims are as empty as their spirits.

> *There are a lot of water vendors out there.*

After Ron married his wife Teresa, they began to look for a church to invest their lives in. Since they came from different denominational backgrounds, they agreed on a compromise: to find a church that either was independent or of a denomination different from the ones they had grown up in. After searching for a while, they settled on one that seemed to have everything they were looking for. The people were very friendly, the church had many different programs and activities going, and the pastor was a dynamic preacher with a charismatic personality. Ron and Teresa were thrilled.

At first everything went fine, but before long their excitement began to fade. Once they became members, they discovered that they were expected to give 20 percent of their income to the church and be at church almost every night attending classes and services and being involved in many different programs. They were coming and going so much that it began to affect Teresa's health.

They backed off and stopped going to so many things. That's when the phone calls started. "You're backsliding. You'd better get back in church or your souls are in danger. You don't want to go to hell, do you?" Ron and Teresa were so worn down emotionally and physically by the constant demands and guilt-tripping that they bought into the warnings and got more involved again.

By this time, they began to notice that many in the congregation regarded their pastor with near-messianic awe and deference. No one ever challenged him or questioned his authority or his teachings in any way, even when he said some things that Ron and Teresa thought were really off-the-wall. "What have we gotten ourselves into?" they wondered.

Teresa's nervous breakdown was the last straw. After she got out of the hospital, they moved across the city and got an unlisted telephone number so the calls would stop. They had become so emotionally and psychologically dependent that breaking with that church was very hard to do and left them deeply hurt and suspicious. Gradually, however, they began to heal. They connected with another church near their new home, a church that preached the Gospel with honesty and integrity. The congregation ministered lovingly to Ron and Teresa in their need, and they have begun worshiping and serving the Lord again. They have a long way to go to completely heal, but at least they now are in a place where they can connect with the true living water.

Don't make the mistake of trading one empty well for another. Do your homework. John tells us:

Dear friends, do not believe every spirit, but test the spirits to see whether they are from God, because many false prophets have gone out into the world. This is how you can recognize the Spirit of God: Every spirit that acknowledges that Jesus Christ has come in the flesh is from God, but every spirit that does not acknowledge Jesus is not from God. This is the spirit of the antichrist, which you have heard is coming and even now is already in the world (1 John 4:1-3).

Connect with people who practice what they preach.

Before you attach yourself to a particular body of believers, check them out. Find out what they believe and make sure it is in line with what you believe. More important, make sure it is in line with what God's Word teaches. Do they exalt Jesus Christ or do they lift up their own agenda? Do their actions match their words? In other words, do they practice what they preach?

Not everyone who preaches in the *name* of Christ possesses the *Spirit* of Christ. What *they* claim to be living water may be nothing but snake oil straight from the "great snake" himself, Satan. That is why we are commanded to test the spirits. Jesus said:

Not everyone who says to me, "Lord, Lord," will enter the kingdom of heaven, but only he who does the will of my Father who is in heaven. Many will say to me on that day, "Lord, Lord, did we not prophesy in your name, and in your name drive out demons and perform many miracles?" Then I will tell them plainly, "I never knew you. Away from me, you evildoers!" (Matthew 7:21-23)

Don't be a loner. You need the regular fellowship and interaction with other believers in a church family. Just be careful who you attach yourself to. Make sure they are attached to the living water of Jesus Christ.

Don't Hoard Your Water

One way to keep your water fresh is to pour it out.

Now that you are connected to the living water that Jesus provides, you need to drink from it daily. Don't worry about running out; He has an everlasting supply. Drink daily through private and family worship, through Bible reading and study, and through prayer. Daily draughts from the well are necessary to keep the water in your spirit clean and pure and fresh and flowing.

Water must flow to stay fresh; otherwise, it stagnates. Remember, that's why the Dead Sea is dead. With no outlet, the water has no place to escape except by evaporation. One way to keep your water fresh is to pour it out. There are people all around you who need to drink from the living water that

174

Jesus gives. You can be their well, their access point. Because Jesus has poured His life into you, you can pour His life—and yours—into others.

Don't hoard your water. Living water is meant to be shared. Sometimes we are so afraid of being hurt again that we want to hold on to the blessings of the water He has given us. The living water of Jesus can't be hoarded. If we try, it will turn sour and stagnant on us.

When the Israelites were in the desert for 40 years after leaving Egypt, God fed them with manna every day. Manna was a daily supply; it could not be hoarded. Each family was to gather each morning only what they needed for that day. The only exception was on the sixth day, when they could gather two-days' worth to cover them across the Sabbath. Those who tried to gather more than one day's supply or who tried to save some until the next day discovered that the sweet-tasting manna spoiled overnight, becoming moldy and maggot-filled.

Like manna, living water is a daily supply, not to be hoarded but to be shared, poured out freely in love and affirmation and compassion and encouragement and service to hurting, thirsty people. Drinking from the living water daily is so important because as we pour out the water that has been poured into us, we need to keep going back to the well for more. It becomes a daily cycle: drink, get filled, pour out; drink, get filled, pour out; drink, get filled, pour out.

The living water is so refreshing that it is tempting simply to say, "I just want to attach to Jesus." That's not what He told us to do. In John 15, Jesus said that He is the Vine and we are the branches, and we must stay attached to Him or else we will dry up and die. Our purpose as branches, however, is not simply to cling to the vine, but to bear fruit. Jesus specifically stated that branches that do not bear fruit will be cut off. In order to bear fruit we must stay attached to the Vine, and if we do stay attached to the Vine, we *will* bear fruit—the fruit of changed lives, ours as well as others'. It's a spiritual principle.

A fast way to become an empty well is to be stingy with your water.

Jesus gives us His living water not so we can hoard it but so that we can pour it out. How do we do that? By opening our hearts to the people and needs around us and responding accordingly. All around you are people with needs that Jesus wants you to fill. That's why He has brought them across your path. If you are hoarding your water, or if you have run out because you're not drinking daily, those folks you were supposed to fill will go away thirsty still. The water you refused to share will start to become stagnant, along with your spirit. One of the fastest ways to become an empty well is by being stingy with the water you have.

We are the skin, the bones, the mouth, the hands, and the feet of Jesus in this world. We are His touch and His love and His compassion. Until He returns visibly and bodily in glory, the only way a lost and dying world can see Jesus is in and through us. How we live, how we love, how we serve, and how we share the love of Jesus with others will determine how well they see Him in us or whether they see Him at all.

Proof of eternal life in us is found in the water we pour out, not the water we hold back. Jesus said:

Drink From the Living Water

Then the King will say to those on his right, "Come, you who are blessed by my Father; take your inheritance, the kingdom prepared for you since the creation of the world. For I was hungry and you gave me something to eat, I was thirsty and you gave me something to drink, I was a stranger and you invited me in, I needed clothes and you clothed me, I was sick and you looked after me, I was in prison and you came to visit me." Then the righteous will answer him, "Lord, when did we see you hungry and feed you, or thirsty and give you something to drink? When did we see you a stranger and invite you in, or needing clothes and clothe you? When did we see you sick or in prison and go to visit you?" The King will reply, "I tell you the truth, whatever you did for one of the least of these brothers of mine, you did for me" (Matthew 25:34-40).

Jesus poured His living water into you for a purpose. His water is meant to be shared. Drink it in daily and pour it out daily. Empty yourself by giving away that which you have received. When you return to the well, you will be filled again. Pour out your water. Let the poured-out life of Jesus flow through you to touch those around you. Then you will be well along the road to healing and wholeness. That road is not a solitary road, however. Your journey to wholeness will not be complete until you learn how to bring others with you.

Chapter Ten

JOURNEY TO WHOLENESS

The Steven Spielberg film, *...batteries not included,* tells the story of a group of lonely tenants in a run-down apartment building whose lives are changed by extraterrestrial visitors. Faced with the imminent loss of their homes by an ambitious and unscrupulous developer who wants to replace their old building with a high-rise office and shopping complex, the tenants try to fight back but feel it is a losing battle.

One night, while everyone is asleep, two small flying saucers zoom into the building. The saucers are themselves "alive"; sentient beings whose "life" is based on electronics rather than biology and on silicon rather than carbon. It is the innate nature of these beings to repair things, and the tenants soon discover that various broken appliances are suddenly working again. Before long, the tenants discover the presence of their visitors and, after an initial period of shock and fear, begin a cautious co-existence with them that grows increasingly friendly.

At one point in the story the "female" saucer gives "birth" to two "baby" saucers. The first one comes out fine and immediately starts zipping and zooming around the room. A few minutes later, the second one comes out ugly, misshapen, and—broken. Lifeless. No lights, no clicking, no whirring. Nothing. The "parents" mourn their stillborn "baby" and give it up for lost.

A short while later, one of the tenants picks up the stillborn saucer, gets his tools, and goes to work. Throughout the night he tinkers and works on the saucer and by morning has repaired it. Coming suddenly to life, it zooms off and is soon reunited with its parents.

Life is a journey from brokenness to wholeness.

Life is a journey from brokenness to wholeness. We all enter life broken, so marred and twisted by sin that we cannot function according to God's design. The spiritual dimension of our being enters this world stillborn. We are all born spiritually dead and remain that way until and unless we are brought to life in Christ. Then and only then do we enter into a relationship with our heavenly Father and begin the journey toward wholeness.

Most people never find wholeness, either because they refuse to admit that they are broken or, if they acknowledge their brokenness, never discover how to get fixed. What prevents people from admitting that they are broken? Any number of things: ignorance, fear, pride, stubbornness, a rebellious spirit.

Journey to Wholeness

Modern society doesn't help any. Our heroes are the strong, resourceful, self-reliant, got-it-all-together John Wayne types who take on the world single-handedly and win. We hold up as a model the independent, self-made, successful individual whose theme song is the old Sinatra tune, "I Did It My Way." Despite the politically correct lip service we give to them, we really have very little room or respect for broken people.

Broken people have no power. They have no influence. They have few resources. Often, they have no dignity, at least in the eyes of the world. Broken people are embarrassing. Broken people possess nothing that the world considers to be of value or worth.

There are two kinds of brokenness. The first is the brokenness we are born with so that we don't "work" right. The second is the brokenness of life we all must experience before we can be made whole. Just as a partially broken bone must be completely broken before it can be set to heal properly, so must we be broken of our pride and self-sufficiency before we can be healed.

Brokenness strips away our facades. It tears down the false walls of pride and self-assurance and bravado that we have erected to keep anyone from seeing the hurting, frightened, cowering child we really are inside. It opens our eyes so we see ourselves as we really are, not as we pretend we are both to ourselves as well as to others. Brokenness comes up to us as we stand proudly on the rock of our self-reliance— and kicks away the stone. It brings us to the end of our own resources so that we will learn to rely on God's resources. Brokenness seeks to turn us from depending on ourselves to depending totally on God. That is why brokenness is where we must start on our road to wholeness.

Before we can be made whole we have to know we are broken.

Before we can be made full we have to know we are empty.

Before we can be made free we have to know we are in bondage.

Before we can be made well we have to know we are sick.

Before we can be made to drink we have to know we are thirsty.

Brokenness brings us down so that when we are at the bottom we will look up.

Brokenness Is the Pathway to Blessedness

What is the key to happiness? Ask that question of the average person on the street and you will get all sorts of answers. Money. Power. Fame. Good health. Good food. A fancy car. A big house. Being loved.

Jesus addressed the same question but came up with very different answers. According to Him and contrary to what the world believes, the pathway to blessedness (happiness) is brokenness. It is only when we are broken that we are in a position to be blessed. Matthew 5:3-10 contains eight statements, commonly known as the "Beatitudes," spoken by Jesus regarding the nature of true happiness. Every one of them refers to a broken person. Consider Jesus' words:

Blessed are the poor in spirit, for theirs is the kingdom of heaven (Matthew 5:3).

Journey to Wholeness

The poor in spirit are broken people who know they have nothing to bring before God; they have no merit of their own with which to claim His favor, but are totally dependent on His grace and mercy. Because they know they have nothing, God will give them everything.

Blessed are those who mourn, for they will be comforted (Matthew 5:4).

Mourners are those who are broken by grief, sorrow, guilt, and regret over not only their own sins but also those of others, knowing that they are an offense to God's holiness. Mourning implies repentance. Only broken people repent, and when they do, God will lift their mourning and comfort their spirits.

Blessed are the meek, for they will inherit the earth (Matthew 5:5).

The meek are broken people too, for they have learned gentleness. Meekness refers to strength deliberately controlled, as with a horse brought under bit and bridle. Gentleness is a quality of the broken because it is contrary to human nature, and only the broken understand its value. In the end, it will be the meek who inherit the earth, not the aggressive and the oppressive.

Blessed are those who hunger and thirst for righteousness, for they will be filled (Matthew 5:6).

Broken people hunger and thirst for righteousness because they know that they have none of their own. Only in Christ do they stand in right relationship with God. The words *hunger* and *thirst* refer not to a gentle tugging ache in the stomach but an intense craving, a life-or-death need for satisfaction. God will feed them the bread of life and the living water.

Blessed are the merciful, for they will be shown mercy (Matthew 5:7).

Only broken people truly know mercy because they also know how badly they need it. Having received mercy from the Lord in the forgiveness of their sins, they find that they can do no less than be merciful to others. Mercy begets mercy.

Blessed are the pure in heart, for they will see God (Matthew 5:8).

Broken people's hearts are pure because they have been through the cleansing waters of forgiveness. They have set their eyes on God and because their hearts' desire is to see Him, God will show Himself to them.

Blessed are the peacemakers, for they will be called sons of God (Matthew 5:9).

Peacemaking goes against our selfish, belligerent nature. Broken people have learned the value of peace and that it is a commodity only God can give. Because they promote peace and seek it at every turn, they reflect the character of God and God is pleased to call them His sons.

Blessed are those who are persecuted because of righteousness, for theirs is the kingdom of heaven (Matthew 5:10).

Broken people have learned that there are higher truths and values than those touted by the world. Consequently, they refuse to conform to the world's mold and the world hates them for it just as it hated their Master and nailed Him to a cross. Because their allegiance is to the King of kings, His kingdom belongs to them.

Brokenness is the pathway to blessedness. There is no other.

The Long Road Home

Our journey to wholeness is a journey that will take a lifetime. In fact, unless Jesus returns first, none of us will complete it this side of the grave. The reason is simple: Our wholeness is in God, and we will never be completely whole until we are literally in His presence in glory. As children of the King we are citizens of heaven and are on the long road home. Each day we live brings us one day closer.

> *Brokenness is the pathway to blessedness.*

Just because we will not achieve full wholeness in this life does not mean that we can't come pretty close. During the journey, we can experience many of the distinctive qualities and blessings of a life that has been transformed from brokenness to wholeness. One of these blessings is the blessing of peace.

Wholeness brings peace to our spirits. Are you at peace today? Peace is not necessarily the absence of conflict but an assured sense of calmness, tranquility, and well-being even in the midst of conflict. This kind of peace is not a clueless and uninformed optimism but a fruit of the Spirit, and as such comes only from God. As Paul wrote to the Philippian church, *"Do not be anxious about anything, but in everything, by*

185

prayer and petition, with thanksgiving, present your requests to God. And the peace of God, which transcends all understanding, will guard your hearts and your minds in Christ Jesus" (Philippians 4:6-7). On the night before He died, Jesus told His disciples, *"Peace I leave with you; my peace I give you. I do not give to you as the world gives. Do not let your hearts be troubled and do not be afraid"* (John 14:27).

Wholeness means being at peace with God.

The peace of wholeness first of all means being at peace with God. The moment you first acknowledged your sinfulness and turned to Christ in faith for forgiveness of your sins, you received peace with God. No more begging, no more striving, no more anxious working on your part and worrying whether or not God is happy with you. Peace with God did away with all that. Now you stand clean and righteous and forgiven on the basis of the blood of Jesus, not a beggar but a beloved son or daughter and a full heir to all of God's riches. There is no more division, no more separation, no more condemning guilt to press you down. You can now come boldly into your Father's throne room and know you will see not an angry scowl but a delighted smile.

Secondly, the peace of wholeness means being at peace with your neighbor. This could be anyone you interact with on any level. For our purposes here, it means especially being at peace with your empty well. Have you made peace with your empty well, at least in your heart? Have you forgiven that person for being empty for you and for hurting you and for rejecting you? Have you let him or her off the hook? Are you willing to live at peace with your empty well even if he or she never shows signs of changing? Colossians 3:15 says, *"Let the peace of Christ rule in your hearts, since as members of one body you were called to peace. And be thankful."* Is Christ's peace ruling in your heart with regard to your empty well?

The peace of wholeness also means being at peace with yourself. Have you forgiven yourself for the years wasted going again and again to your empty well? Have you forgiven yourself for being an empty well and for hurting the people who depend on you? Have you come to a healthy self-image and sense of self-worth based not on your own merits but on what Christ has done for you and in you? Are you at peace with allowing Him to mold and shape you into the person He wants you to be? Have you taken control of your life by releasing control to Him? Are you at peace letting Jesus handle the remote?

Wholeness also brings the peace of contentment. Are you content with your life and situation as they are today? Contentment does not mean that you no longer have any life goals to strive for, but it does mean that you are no longer driven by ambition or by the need for attention or recognition. Are you content in the knowledge that even if you are not where you want to be, you are at least on the journey?

Wholeness brings the peace of a mind, body, and spirit that are unified and not fragmented, working in harmony rather than dissonance. Are you in conflict with yourself in any way or are you in internal harmony? Are you growing in integrity as each of the disparate parts of your life become more integrated into a unified whole?

Finally, wholeness brings the peace of resting in the love and care of God and being able to say, "I have everything I need."

The journey to wholeness should be a continuing progression from chaos to calm, from dissonance to harmony, from fragmentation to integration, from the arid waste of the empty well to the abundant waters of God's river of life.

The Long Road Is Not a Lonely Road

The road home may be long but it shouldn't be lonely. First of all, we have the Spirit of God with us as our constant companion and guide. He knows every step of the way, every twist and every turn, every place where it will be easy to get off track and head in the wrong direction. He will always be there to strengthen us when we tire, pick us up when we fall, encourage us when we falter, and fill us when we open up. He is the source of our living water, which is our nourishment and strength for the journey.

We cannot make the journey to wholeness without bringing wholeness to others.

Second, the road should not be lonely because we will not be walking it alone. We are bound to meet other travelers along the way. Some of them will be closer to wholeness than we are, and we can draw from their wells and learn from them. Others will be behind us in the way, and we need to come alongside, let them drink from our wells, and then bring them along with us.

There is no way we can truly make the journey to wholeness without bringing wholeness to others. As we learn to let the living water of the Lord pour into us and fill us and transform us, it is bound to overflow and spill over into the lives of the people around us. We do not live in a vacuum. It is impossible for us to find complete emotional fulfillment without it affecting and changing other people.

All around you are people who need living water from your well to satisfy their thirsty hearts. Living water is meant to be shared; it *must* be shared. God did not touch you and change you and lift you out of your empty well syndrome and fill you up merely for your own pleasure and enjoyment. No, He wants you to "pay it forward" so someone else can be blessed by the water you have received. The power of the living water to change lives is so formidable that someday you may even be able to "pay it backward," reconnect with your empty well (or connect for the first time) and enter into the mutual full well relationship you always dreamed of.

Your journey to wholeness means that you will do everything in your power to be a full well for the people who depend on you as well as for any others God places in your path. True success is never accidental; it comes only with deliberate planning and hard work.

Coach John R. Wooden, Head Basketball Coach Emeritus at UCLA, ESPN's "Coach of the Year," Presidential Medal of Freedom recipient, and the winningest college basketball coach in history said:

> Success is peace of mind, a direct result of self-satisfaction in knowing that you did your best to become the best that you are capable of becoming, and not just in a physical way: seek ye first the kingdom and His righteousness and all these things will be yours as well.

Someone is looking to you for fresh, life-giving water to nourish his or her thirsty heart. Are you ready to be the full well that person needs?

Your simple love, your simple heart, your simple words of affirmation may be all that a person needs to become everything that he or she can be.

Let your water flow!

PRAYERS FOR YOU

Part One: Into the Desert—The Nurturing Years

Chapter One: All You Need Is Love

"Lord, I need love so badly in my heart and my life. Please begin the process of teaching me what it means to love and be loved. Lord, I need to know a pure and genuine love. I'm not sure what real love is anyway. The Bible says that perfect love casts out all fears. Lord, I need to know perfect love. Amen."

Chapter Two: Daddy, I'm Begging for Your Attention!

"Lord, I ask that You help me to see myself. I just want to be honest with myself and have the ability to recognize the truth in all areas of my life. I don't want to live a lie but to live a life of truth. Help me to see why I do the things that I do and to recognize if I am a full or empty well. I am tired of being insecure and begging for others' attention. I want to be free! Amen."

Chapter Three: Do You Even See Me?

"Lord, today the cycle stops. I am not invisible. My future does not depend on what others think, and it's time to shake some things off of my life and walk into my destiny. Lord, help me to see all those who have been invisible to me and show me how I can make a difference in their lives. Amen."

Part Two: Turning Point—Self-Discovery

Chapter Four: My Well Is Empty

"Lord, this could be one of the most difficult things that I have ever done in my life. I need Your help to make changes in my life. This affects the very core of my being; this is one of the most tender parts of my life. Help me to release my empty well and find new ones. Help me with the guilt and hurt that I am dealing with right now. I don't know if I can do this alone. Lord, I need Your help. Give me the strength to release my empty well in love not hate. I am ready to be full. Lord, I now pray for my empty well, and I ask that You teach him (or her) how to love and be full for himself. I ask that You bless him and make him whole because I've tried for years and it has not worked. Lord, I'm trusting You for the both of us. Amen."

Chapter Five: Give Me the Remote

"Lord, I am tired of living my life through someone else's eyes. It is time for me to be me! I wish that my well would change—I want my well to change—but I

realize that I can't fix my well. So now I release this per-
son to You, and I am ready to become the change that
I need to be. Amen."

Chapter Six: Let It Go

True forgiveness requires more than just saying a prayer. If you are genuinely serious about forgiving your well, then I suggest you do the following: Write it down. Go all the way back to the beginning and write down everything that this empty well person has done to hurt you. Just let it pour out of your soul. You will be amazed at how many hurts, wrongs, and pains you have swept under the rug. This process deals with the truth of all the injustices that you have endured. Take your time and be thorough. Don't expect to do it all in one day; it may take months. After you're finished writing, imagine this person or persons sitting on a couch in front of you, and read to them what you wrote. You could make it like a letter. [Note: Do *not* read this to anyone. You are doing this for yourself.] After you are finished reading, pray a prayer that goes like this: "Lord, I want to be free from the pain and hate in my life and even from those people who have hurt me. I choose to let it all go right now. I give it to You, and I forgive them of every-thing. I vow to never pick up anything that I let go here today. I choose to let them off the hook for any wrong they commit-ted. I will live a life of forgiveness for the rest of my life. Amen." Now take that paper, or letter, and burn it as a sym-bol of destroying your past so you can successfully continue your journey to wholeness.

Part Three: Out of the Desert—
The Journey to Healing and Freedom

Chapter Seven: You Have a Father

"Lord, as I am learning to live a life of forgiveness and healing, I ask that You fill the love-shaped hole that's on the inside of me. I want to be a well of love to those who need it. Amen."

Chapter Eight: No More Begging

"Lord, I want to be a free-flowing well to others. Help me to realize that I am a child of the King of kings and Lord of lords. I am not a beggar! I was created for greatness, and I have an obligation to let the living water flow out of my life. Help me to be full and ever flowing. Amen."

Chapter Nine: Drink From the Living Water (Prayer of Salvation)

"Dear Lord Jesus, come into my life and forgive me of all my shortcomings and sin, so I can experience the true love of God in my life. I want to know You, Jesus, and truly understand Your love. Amen."

If you prayed this very simple and short prayer, Jesus has just come into your life. There is a book in heaven called the Lamb's Book of Life, and when you prayed that prayer you became a true child of God. Your name was written in that book. And when the day comes that you leave your body, your spirit will stand before the gatekeeper of heaven and he will ask if your name is in the book. You can now say, "My name is in that book because I asked Jesus into my life." The gatekeeper will say, "Enter in, thou good and faithful servant."

Prayers for You

Chapter Ten: Journey to Wholeness (The Serenity Prayer)

*"God, grant me the **serenity** to accept the things I cannot change; courage to change the things I can; and wisdom to know the difference....Amen."*

EMPTYWELL.COM

*E*mptywell.com is the place to go to get the consistent encouragement you need to face the empty wells in your life. The process of forgiving someone and letting go of the hurt is vital to your well-being. It is so important that you *not* pick up the pains you have released. Keep in mind that simply forgiving your well does not mean that your well has changed. The change is with *you*, not him or her. So often we think that because we are changing, those around us must change also. But that is rarely the case. You are not invincible or exempt from being hurt again. It is quite possible that as soon as you think you have a handle on this, you could get blindsided with the very issues you have been dealing with. Join us at Emptywell.com for a specialized chat room and email encouragement to help you stay on course.

COMING SOON...

A Workbook/Journal

A Workbook/Journal for Teens

A Workbook/Journal for Married Couples

A Workbook/Journal for Leaders

ABOUT THE AUTHOR

No stranger to ministry, Mark Leonard has served for upwards of 22 years in various roles. He began by running sound in his father's church, and eventually he moved up to develop a national television ministry for Heritage Christian Center. As a director and producer, he has worked on more than 2,500 television programs. Mark also has used his creative talents in writing, directing, and producing 42 original stage productions viewed by over a half million people. Today Mark Leonard serves as a youth pastor of more than 700 young people in Denver, Colorado.